MASCULINE REVOLUTION

A Journey To Reclaim Your Masculine Essence Through The Power Of Archetypes

By Dr. RB Hernández-Cruz

La Farfalla Publishing House 2023

I dedicate this book to...
All the boys and men who have had similar experiences and whose becoming a man was very difficult. Here's to you: you are not alone.
Donna, my editor, who saw the value of this content and helped me reshape the book to serve a broader audience.
Those men, Papi, my Stepfather, Uncle Mario, Jose, Pastor Dan, Enrique, Danila & Fred, who have been vital in my becoming.
Bernadette and Matthew, my inspiration and motivation for getting this book out to the world.
Finally, my mom and other mothers who have allowed masculine archetypal energies to help them raise their children as single mothers.
Thank you, Mom!

"The masculine archetype is not a matter of anatomy, but of consciousness."
Carl Jung, The Collected Works of C.G. Jung, Volume 9, Part 1:
The Archetypes and the Collective Unconscious

Introduction

Have you struggled greatly with masculinity for what seems like forever? Have you struggled with perceiving what it means to be masculine in the eyes of society, family, and friends?

Have you always felt that there was more to masculinity and that it's a layered thing with many dimensions, as opposed to being a one-dimensional, one-size-fits-all dynamic?

If so, you're certainly not alone. I've been there, and countless men have been, and continue to be, in your position.

This book is written precisely for you and others just like you, from my perspective as somebody who had similar struggles to yours and had to revise his perspective on the subject - the perspective that society pushed on him and everyone else around him.

It all started when I was gifted the book "King, Warrior, Magician, and Lover" by Robert Moore and Douglas Gillette.

Little did I know that this book would take me on an extraordinary journey when I got it. It was like stepping into a whole new world.

This book opened a door that had been shut tight for years and years. As I delved into the pages, it felt as if I were strolling through a meadow, following a dirt path that led me straight into a mysterious, enchanting forest. Deep within those woods was a dormant part of me, waiting to be awakened.

I remember reading this book on a plane, heading to Denver for a big interview. The timing couldn't have been more perfect. It was as if this journey of self-discovery and growth synchronized with the physical adventure I was about to embark upon.

As I absorbed the wisdom within those pages, it felt like I was giving life to that inner boy who had been yearning to grow up, fulfill his destiny, and step into his true manhood. It was a most profound process for me. Carl Jung called it individuation, which became my goal—finding and embracing my archetypal masculine energy in all its glory.

I hope this book can be for you what "King, Warrior, Magician, and Lover" was for me.

The main goal of this book is to delve into the fascinating topic of masculine archetypal energy, particularly as it manifests in men, including those who identify as gay. By exploring this subject, we aim to bring more clarity and understanding to the diverse expressions of masculinity.

As I reflect on my own life, I can't help but acknowledge the significant roles played by my father, stepfather, and uncle in exemplifying masculine archetypal energies. Their influence has shaped my journey, and I'm eager and excited to share those experiences with you.

Let's get started.

Table of Contents

Dr. R B Hernández-Cruz

Chapter 1: Discovering & Deciphering Masculinity – My Story

IN MY CLINICAL WORK as a psychologist, I have observed a concerning scarcity of mature masculine archetypes in today's world. This observation has sparked my curiosity and motivated me to delve deeper into this subject.

Drawing from the invaluable insights of Carl Jung's Collected Works and other Jungian perspectives, I aim to comprehensively analyze masculinity and masculine archetypes.

---

1. https://unsplash.com/@birminghammuseumstrust

Carl Jung, a renowned Swiss psychiatrist and psychoanalyst, explored the concept of archetypes, such as the ones we will explore in this book, as universal patterns within each of us.

I hope to shed light on the traditional masculine archetypes and how they have evolved by examining Jung's works and other Jungian perspectives. The book will explore the archetypes explored in "Warrior, the King, the Lover, and the Magician" by Robert Moore and Douglas Gillette, which I brought up in the introduction, among other archetypes observed in various cultures and mythologies.

Let's touch on these archetypes briefly, so you have some understanding of them right off the bat:

1) **King**: The king archetype represents the mature and benevolent ruler, the wise leader who governs with integrity and compassion. He symbolizes authority, responsibility, and the ability to provide a sense of order and purpose. A man who embodies the king archetype is confident in his decisions, exercises self-discipline, and prioritizes the well-being of his community.

2) **Warrior**: The warrior archetype embodies strength, courage, and a readiness to take decisive action. This archetype is not solely about physical combat but encompasses the inner battle against adversity, fear, and injustice. A man with a developed Warrior archetype is assertive, disciplined, and driven by a code of honor. He protects what is meaningful to him and fights for his values and principles.

3) **Magician**: The magician archetype represents wisdom, insight, and transformation. He delves into the mysteries of life, seeking to understand the deeper truths and hidden aspects of reality. The magician is connected to intuition, creativity, and the ability to bring about positive change through knowledge and inner growth.

4) **Lover**: The lover archetype is associated with passion, sensuality, and emotional depth. This aspect of masculinity involves connecting deeply with others and experiencing profound love and joy. The lover is attuned to beauty, art, and the pleasures of life. This archetype encourages men to embrace their emotions, be vulnerable, and form authentic connections with others.

You are correct if you noticed that these masculine archetypes described are all positive. I mentioned only their positive sides. There is what is described as the *shadow* aspect to them, or the negative side, which I will touch upon.

Before we move on with this particular chapter, I have to mention that I will initially explore three out of the four masculine archetypes above and described by Robert Moore and Douglas Gillette, leaving out the warrior archetype.

Please note that excluding this archetype does not undermine its significance or its impact on my life, far from it. However, in my journey, I will focus on the men, as I mentioned above, who have embodied the masculine archetypes I cover. I haven't encountered someone who embodied the warrior energy for me.

As far as my example goes, however, I've come to recognize the traits and characteristics of this warrior masculine archetype in myself, my way of being and functioning. I've had to defend my sexual orientation, beliefs, and masculinity in many ways. You might sense the warrior archetype in the background as the book unravels. Most likely, I will dedicate time to the warrior in another book – stay tuned.

Moving on, it is essential to acknowledge that societal expectations and norms regarding gender roles have evolved, leading to new expressions of masculinity and challenging the traditional archetypes. By exploring contemporary male experiences and narratives, I aim to present a nuanced view of masculinity that embraces a broader, more inclusive understanding of what it means to be a man in the modern world.

As I weave together my personal and clinical experiences along with Jungian insights, I envision a narrative that transcends gender and sexual orientation, inviting readers from all walks of life to resonate with the themes explored within the pages of this book. While the focus is on masculinity, the insights offered will be valuable for individuals of all genders, in whatever way one's gender is identified or presented, as they navigate their identities and relationships in a complex and diverse society.

By providing a safe space for readers to reflect on their own experiences and perspectives, I aspire to foster understanding and empathy toward the struggles and aspirations of others. Through this exploration of masculinity, I hope to encourage meaningful conversations and connections among individuals, fostering a more compassionate and understanding world.

This book will not only aim to analyze the archetypes but also offer practical guidance on how readers can integrate and balance different aspects of masculinity within themselves. Emphasizing the importance of self-awareness and emotional intelligence, I hope to empower readers to cultivate a healthier and more authentic expression of their masculine qualities.

Ultimately, my goal is for this book to be a catalyst for personal growth and societal transformation, encouraging you, the reader, to explore your own identity, forge meaningful connections with others, and contribute to a world where diverse expressions of masculinity are embraced and celebrated.

I want this particular chapter to act as a solid foundation upon which we can build the rest of the book. The best foundation we could have for the book's subject matter is concise coverage of the changing landscape of masculinity in society and the changing roles of men today.

I'll outline my personal story first so you're at the very least acquainted with essential elements of my journey. Once you're done reading my personal story, I hope you will be better placed to see where I'm coming from and better understand my perspectives as I express them.

Let's get started.

Perth, Australia

MY JOURNEY GOES BACK to 1992, when my life took a dramatic turn and set me on a path of transformation I could never have imagined.

It all started when I felt this undeniable pull to travel to Australia and become a youth pastor for a cozy little church nestled deep in Carmel, east of Perth, Western Australia.

Now, to embark on this journey of self-discovery, I had to leave behind everything familiar – my family and friends. I ventured across the globe on what, years later, I discovered to be referred to as the *Hero's Journey*.

Settling in and getting acclimated to a brand-new place halfway across the earth, especially one where I knew nobody and was thoroughly unfamiliar with the culture, wasn't easy by any stretch.

It was on this journey that I would come to terms with being a gay person. I had never come out to anyone, not my loved ones, and not even me. To complicate matters more, I would work as a youth pastor and a teacher at the church's high school.

I was at a loss for what to do and asked myself many questions during my time there.

"As a clergyperson, should I socialize and get close to these people?"

"Is my sexual orientation going to be a problem?"

"Will I be able to trust anyone enough to tell them my truth, especially given that I haven't even told my mom, the rest of my family, and those I love?"

I wanted to get close but didn't know how.

But over the next six months, I gradually let down my mask, becoming more open to these Aussies and them to me. I lived by myself, grateful that it gave me time to reflect. I pondered and meditated deeply on who I was to these people and myself.

It took me some time before I could use the word "gay" confidently as part of my identity. It was part of my experiences on the other side of the world that I struggled with accepting my sexuality. The thoughts, the feelings, and the strong desires in my heart caused me much guilt. After all, I was the youth pastor, so I felt compelled to be extra careful not to fall into scandal. Most of all, I was still a virgin, inexperienced, and I don't know if this made things a little easier.

It wasn't until I opened up to my boss, Pastor Dan, that I truly started to come into my own as my own man.

Coming Out

PASTOR DAN WAS MY IMMEDIATE senior, my "boss," so to speak. He was the head pastor of the small Perth church to which I had been assigned.

He was also the first person to whom I confessed my homosexuality.

When I came out to him, I instantly expected him to judge me.

He did not.

And right there and then, I became convinced that saints do, indeed, exist.

Instead of judging me or trying to "change" me, Pastor Dan cared for me and understood me. For my own sake, he advised me to remain celibate and do everything I could to avoid scandal.

Better yet, he promised me that he would struggle with me. Having never met a gay individual, he asked me many questions in an attempt to understand what it meant to be gay. He even asked me if I was attracted to his two small sons and whether he should be concerned.

Looking back, it's obvious that Pastor Dan was a great example of healthy masculinity.

How so?

For starters, instead of imposing any beliefs, fears, or worries, he may have had on the issue of homosexuality, he chose to try and understand me as a gay individual to the best of his ability.

Instead of using his senior position to perhaps try and have me conform to any beliefs that he and his peers may have had on the issue, he decided to let me be my person.

Instead of immediately scrambling to conclusions and perceptions that others/society may have had on homosexuality, a subject he had very little knowledge and experience in, especially given that he had never met a gay person before, he chose to first educate himself as well as he could on the subject, through me.

Pastor Dan chose to understand and accommodate instead of judge and impose. And in that regard, he was a phenomenal example of healthy masculinity.

I need to insist, especially given that this was way back in the 90s when homosexuality was still heavily frowned upon, especially among religious circles and spaces, that he could have easily judged me, perhaps even become hostile. But instead, he chose to guide me with genuine wisdom and compassion. He constantly pushed me to grow by asking thought-provoking questions and helping me gain more knowledge. He did this special thing for me, playing a massive role in my becoming a man.

But even with Pastor Dan walking with me every step of the way and being a listening ear, I still struggled a lot as I shuffled toward the realm of mature masculinity.

I especially had major struggles with personal restraint, something that Pastor Dan wisely recommended I exercise vigilantly.

Heavy Struggles with Personal Restraint

ALLOW ME TO REFERENCE alchemy for a bit before I carry on.

If you delve into the fascinating world of alchemy, you'll come across symbols representing different elements. One symbol that stands out is the symbol for fire, which is closely connected to a process called *calicinatio or* calcination.

Calcination is a method of burning certain elements to either purify them or dry them out from other elements. The fire symbol in alchemy is a psychological symbol for restraining oneself from giving in to temptations and passions. It's all about self-control and resisting those urges that may lead us astray.

Which leads me to this...

Beginning my sexual experience, there would have been a truly foolish idea that would only have served to ruin my experience. I would have been robbed of the joy and love I felt from all those who welcomed me into their homes and lives.

To be clear, I was often burning with desire with the many attractive men around me. In both the church and the city where I lived, I experienced the flames of desire and longing. Aussie guys are hot!

Luckily, I had the lovely Pastor Dan by my side, guiding me patiently through these intense flames of desire. Many people may argue that this was unhealthy, that I was being enabled in repression, but please understand that this was when I'd just moved to Perth to help a small church and school. Other things were way more important to me at the time than physically exploring my sexuality. Yes, I could have begun living a gay life earlier, but in retrospect, I'm ever so glad that I waited.

During the entire time, Pastor Dan offered me his friendship, a listening ear, and unconditional support. He was that rare soul that would be there for me, listening keenly and offering help even if I were to call at 3 a.m. That experience made me feel like God was with me, acting as a loving father, a source of positive energy, and a healthy male figure.

But not all this could have prepared me for the experience of coming out to my loved ones. My mom, specifically.

Coming Out... Again

I NEED TO PROVIDE A bit of a preamble before we get to the moment I come out to my mom.

It took me a long time to come to terms with something about myself that I had been pushing aside for years. After much soul-searching, I could no longer ignore or hide my attraction to men. It was a part of me that I needed to acknowledge and accept. Luckily, I found a safe and supportive environment in Australia that allowed me to go through this process.

At that time, my pastor was the only person who knew I was gay. Eventually, I decided to open up to a young woman I had been involved with before my trip to Australia. And later, when my mother visited me in Perth, I found the courage to have a heart-to-heart with her.

It was quite surreal when I "came out" to my mother. My younger sister, who had accompanied my mother on this trip, was engrossed in a TV show in our hotel room while my mom and I had a conversation outside in a rental car on a blustery night in Cairns. It was the perfect opportunity to share my true self with her. All the inner work I had done to accept and integrate this part of my identity finally came to the surface.

During my time in Australia, I had bought into this idea that I could somehow be "healed" and change my sexual preference to fit society's idea of a "God-loving" straight man. So, I told my mother about it, thinking she might understand. She was, understandably, taken aback.

She asked questions like whether being gay resulted from my father leaving us, if something traumatic had happened to me as a child, or even if my father was homosexual. She just wanted some explanation that made sense to her. I can only imagine how challenging it must have been for her to grasp this new reality. Suddenly, her son, who had left just a year before, seemed so unfamiliar and, in her eyes, perhaps even repulsive or shocking.

It was a difficult conversation, but I could tell my mom was genuinely trying to understand and come to terms with this new information. And I truly appreciated her effort at the time, even though it was undoubtedly a lot for her to process.

I also couldn't help but feel great appreciation for Pastor Dan at the moment, the man who had been so instrumental in me accepting myself for who I was and without whom I would never have had the courage to come out to my mother and loved ones and have that heavy load lifted from my soul.

And it's why I embraced it wholeheartedly when I got to do what he did for me to multiple young men who grew up without fathers.

I Get to Become Pastor Dan

AFTER I LEFT PERTH, Australia, and moved back to the U.S., I had the opportunity to work with juvenile offenders.

While working with these juvenile offenders, particularly in Springfield, Massachusetts, I encountered many young men who grew up without fathers. They had a whole different perspective on life. They focused on stealing, envying others, and even resorting to violence if it meant protecting their corner in the drug trade. They were just kids but made more money than I could imagine. It was eye-opening.

I felt a calling, a deep desire to tap into my masculine energy and offer it to these young men. I wanted them to benefit from it, to see a different path.

But here's the thing: even though I'm of Cuban descent, they saw me as "too White" because of how I carried myself. My pants fit me properly, unlike theirs, which were several sizes too big. I was gay to them, and they didn't want a gay, young, White man telling them how to live their lives. It was challenging, but I was determined to break those barriers and show them that I genuinely cared about their well-being. I wanted to guide them toward a better life. It wasn't about being White, Black, or any other label. It was about tapping into our inner selves and our true potential as men.

When I first saw them, I admit I had some preconceived notions and was tempted, because of fear, to call them rats, just like my ex at the time did, in his concern for my safety.

But instead, something inside me urged me to give them a chance and hear their stories without judgment. I decided to be there for them through their tension, fears, insults, and even their attempts at flirting.

It was quite a task. My supervisor told me multiple times that I was playing the role of both a mother and a father to these young ones, which turned out to be quite therapeutic. I found myself nurturing and guiding, like a father figure they never had. It wasn't easy, in any case. The responsibility was immense and overwhelming. However, I took it on, and with time, they started accepting me.

They needed someone to guide and mentor them, helping them grow into mature men.

I will wrap up my account of easing into my masculinity here. I'm pretty sure you're now familiar with a few cornerstones as far as my journey to discovering and deciphering masculinity goes.

But before we get into dissecting and exploring the different kinds of masculine archetypes, I feel I must touch on something that afflicts countless men: living with "boy psychology" even as grown men, and deep down wanting to connect with their inner man, as opposed to their inner boy.

I've struggled mightily with this. Many of my clients have struggled greatly with this as well. You're perhaps struggling with this yourself, as well as others that you may know.

Let's look at this particular subject in some depth. Once we've covered it, we can use it and the content covered in this chapter as a springboard to dive into the varied masculine archetypes.

The "Boy Psychology" Phenomenon

IN MODERN SOCIETY, the role of fathers and father figures in nurturing and guiding young boys into mature men has declined and is an ongoing challenge.

Many men today grew up without positive male role models, and this absence has contributed to what is often referred to as 'boy psychology' among depth psychologists.

Even as adults, many of us still carry certain emotional and behavioral patterns reminiscent of our younger, less mature selves. These patterns may include a reluctance to take on responsibilities, avoiding vulnerability, and difficulty forming meaningful and lasting connections.

Reasons Behind the "Boy Psychology" Phenomenon

ONE KEY REASON BEHIND this 'boy psychology' is the lack of healthy father figures during crucial developmental stages.

Boys may struggle to learn essential life skills and emotional intelligence without proper guidance and mentorship. Consequently, we may carry unresolved emotional baggage into adulthood, hindering our personal growth and impacting our relationships with others.

Yet another reason is that all too often, we, as men, are told that we need to embrace our feminine side and be more "metrosexual," so to speak. This has led many of us to struggle greatly with the unfamiliar feminine energy, often feeling overwhelmed and unable to tap into our masculine energy. This keeps us in a perpetual state of boyhood since we're unable to properly tap into the masculine energy necessary to graduate from boyhood to manhood.

There's an interesting phenomenon that I have come across as I go back and forth with my clients in my practice:

I've noticed that many husbands act more like their wife's sons than their partners. They feel lost and without direction, constantly being told what to do and how to do it by their wives. Many wives run their households without their husband's support, only to take on the role of supermoms.

A huge reason for this, I have found, is that these men have been impressed upon, time and time again by society as well as their wives, to embrace their feminine side... to be less "hard" and manly, and to allow their vulnerable side to the surface more often. But in their efforts to do so, the entire dynamic gets too skewed to the feminine side, and they lose touch with their equally essential masculine side. They tap into their masculine energy less and less, leading them to become more and more like docile little boys as time passes.

Eventually, they relinquish their natural desire for leadership and become content to be led by their more assertive wives, who, on the contrary, have been pressured to cultivate their masculine energy and tap more into that power and essence inside them. I have experienced and believe this creates an imbalance between men and women.

If you've watched the sitcom "Everyone Loves Raymond," you'll see the "boy psychology" fully displayed.

The Raymond character acted like a boy, while his wife's character was depicted as nagging, upset, uptight, and running the household. In addition, Raymond's mother often interfered in the marriage, further keeping him as a boy. The relationship triad portrayed Raymond as the poor victim caught in the middle.

Such is the case for many men in today's society.

Breaking Free and Connecting with Our Inner Man

WE ALL DEEPLY YEARN to connect with our inner, mature masculine energy. And this is especially so for those of us still stuck in our boy psychology for various reasons. This yearning to connect with this energy signifies a deep desire for growth and personal transformation.

Like all individuals, men need to understand themselves, cultivate self-awareness, and embrace their full potential. This inner journey involves acknowledging and addressing past wounds, developing emotional resilience, and learning to embrace vulnerability as a strength rather than a weakness.

With this in mind, how do we break free from 'boy psychology' and connect with our healthy, mature masculine energy?

To break free from the limitations of 'boy psychology,' we must actively seek out positive male role models and male mentors who can guide us on our journey toward mature masculinity.

These mentors can provide valuable insights, support, and constructive feedback, helping us to explore our emotions in ways that we haven't before or in ways that we've felt dissuaded from applying, understand our patterns, and navigate the complexities of life with greater confidence.

Furthermore, cultivating emotional intelligence is critical to transitioning from 'boy psychology' to mature masculinity. Emotional intelligence involves recognizing and understanding one's emotions and those of others, empathizing with different perspectives, and effectively communicating and managing feelings. By developing emotional intelligence, we can forge deeper connections with others, leading to more fulfilling relationships and a greater sense of purpose in life. Again, positive masculine mentors can help us greatly on this journey. Therapists, too, can help here, especially if you feel your issues dealing with emotions are deeply rooted.

Additionally, embracing vulnerability is an essential step in personal growth. I'll talk about this one often throughout the book. Even as society imposes upon us to tap into our feminine side, it has often conditioned us to suppress vulnerability and emotions, portraying it as a sign of weakness.

However, true strength lies in the courage to be open and authentic, to express our feelings, fears, and aspirations without fear of judgment. Embracing vulnerability fosters genuine connections, belonging, and acceptance.

We must also challenge societal stereotypes and expectations surrounding masculinity. This is yet another aspect that I'll touch on often as we go along. The traditional notion of masculinity as stoic, dominant, and unemotional is outdated and limiting, as you'll see from my accounts and examples. Embracing a broader understanding of masculinity allows us, as men, to explore and express a broader range of emotions, interests, and traits without feeling confined by rigid norms.

With everything we've covered thus far, we're ready to get into the various masculine archetypes. However, before we get into the next chapter, I'd like to leave some questions at the end of this chapter.

Please take a few minutes to answer them as concisely as possible. This may help you discover more about yourself and your journey to masculinity.

Here are a few questions to ponder and answer before we get to explore the varied masculine archetypes:

Have you taken a huge jump/risk that perhaps separated you from your family and/or everything familiar to you? What was it? What compelled you to take the jump?

Have you struggled with desires, cravings, and longings that you knew then or now are aware of that you shouldn't act upon in your journey to understanding and embracing yourself? Have you had the fortune of having somebody willing to help you as you grappled with these desires, as I did? What were these desires? Who was that person? How did you cope? Write all of this down.

What is something you've perhaps struggled to come out with and confess to your loved ones that you felt would undercut their perception of you? What was their reaction when you finally did? Do you wish they'd reacted differently? Do you harbor any bad memories or experiences from it that you haven't addressed yet?

Do you struggle with being expected/pushed to tap into an energy that was not yours? Have you felt this was wrong, even though society keeps pushing it onto you and others like yourself? What is your gripe with it, specifically? Do you think it's necessary to tap into masculine energy based on your examples and that of family/ friends?

With these questions answered, use the journaling prompts below to write about anything and everything that's been evoked in you from the contents of this chapter.

If you have any pushback or criticism of my perspectives, write these down and do your best to explain why you feel this way. Then, once you're done with this book, return to these and see if you still have the same opinion(s). I think it is important to have this dialogue, which can be emotionally difficult.

Chapter 2: The Father Archetype

Photo by Jan Kopriva

Understanding the Concept of Archetypes

Before we get into three of the four archetypes we touched on in the previous chapter, I want to explore the father archetype first. This will provide a proper foundation for covering the other masculine archetypes in this book.

But before we explore this particular archetype, I feel it is very important to first explore the concept of archetypes as a whole.

You already have a very good idea of what archetypes connote, given I touched on the four archetypes in the previous chapter and explained what each means. However, providing some more backdrop will help you comprehend the concept of archetypes even better.

Let's get to it...

The term archetypes can be found in the early writings of the ancient philosopher Philo Judaeus.

Philo Judaeus, commonly known as Philo of Alexandria, was an influential ancient philosopher who lived during the first century CE. He was a Hellenistic Jewish philosopher born in Alexandria, Egypt. He is best known for attempting to reconcile Jewish religious teachings with Greek philosophical thought, particularly with Platonism and Stoicism. Philo's writings, primarily in Greek, explored various topics, including ethics, metaphysics, and the nature of God. It is in the nature of God's writings that he spoke about archetypes avidly.

In the 2,000 years since then, there have been many references to archetypes, especially in Platonic philosophy.

The archetypes are described as "types of energy" with a consciousness or life of their own, which influence us. These forms of energy come from the depths of the unconscious.

They take the shape of familiar roles or beings to express themselves. An archetype's expression is not specific to any culture but encompasses all cultures and includes every human experience.

Common forms the archetypes use are, for example, the "mother" and "father" roles or forms of expression. Part of the experience of being human is to have a mother and father, and so these roles, forms, or ways of being become energies or archetypes.

Now that you have an even deeper idea of what the concept of archetypes is and what it is rooted in, I'll outline the purpose and emphasis of this chapter.

Outlining the Goal and Purpose of this Chapter

WHAT I AM MOST CONCERNED with in this chapter, and a point I'd like to stress, is the importance of the father archetype when discussing the mature masculine energy in masculinity.

The father archetype is one form of the collective masculine archetype. A critical function of the father archetype, as expressed in a human father, is to guide the child in eventually exercising his masculinity. Generally, whenever father stereotypes are mentioned, and the healthy father is discussed, an expression of the archetype is present.

In an ideal development, when the child's ego develops sufficient consciousness and can appropriately attach to the parents, the mother and father roles or archetypes become differentiated and manifest; that is, they become conscious. Continually, the father-child relationship emerges and strengthens.

A boy, in particular, undergoes a significant mental shift as he transitions from primarily identifying with his mother to forming a stronger identification with his father. This transition is a natural and essential part of the child's mental and emotional growth. It enables the child to model and internalize the qualities and values typically associated with the father archetype. This is also despite a developing sexual orientation.

This shift in identification allows the child to develop a sense of self that is influenced by their father's characteristics and provides a solid foundation for healthy mental and emotional development and a well-rounded personality.

If the paragraphs above seem a bit technical, then the basic idea I'm trying to convey is that the son gradually sees himself as being more like his dad since he is also male. This is an important part of masculine development in boys.

I specify "boys" because, first of all, this work will focus on boys and the integration of masculinity, with the result of becoming a healthy adult male. Secondly, I think girls also develop masculine energy, integrating healthy masculinity anchored on courage, bravery, and assertiveness as they become healthy adult females with their responsibilities.

Let's explore my experiences to illustrate the aspects and elements I've touched on thus far.

Failing to Identify with My Father & Thus My Masculinity – My Story

THE FIRST COMMENTS I remember my mother making concerning my father were not positive. Let me start from there.

She instructed my siblings and me to respect our father and never say anything negative about him. But she, on the other hand, did not have to follow this rule. When viewing my father through my mother's eyes, I saw a weak man who didn't stand up to his mother and defend his wife—my mother.

Because I experienced my father through my mother's descriptions of him, in my childish eyes, my father was not someone I could be proud of or want to emulate.

It is no wonder that when relatives said I looked like my father, I would quickly say that I didn't. My embarrassment at being compared to my father had serious consequences. Not allowing myself to identify with him, I also blocked myself from being connected to my masculinity. I continued to view my mother as more admirable, which prolonged my identification with her.

For a long time, I could not identify with my father. There was much shame in being compared to him. I wanted to win the favor of my mother by being more like her rather than win her over, as discussed earlier.

As is apparent, this caused problems down the line, and I had to adopt a longer, more complicated path to identifying with my masculinity.

Speaking of masculinity, the vital question is, what do I mean by masculinity? What do I define it as? We explore this one next.

My Definition of Masculinity

IN THIS BOOK, MASCULINITY is defined as traits, or better yet, qualities that are seen and defined across cultures, as well as genders, with some minor differences.

For example, in classical Greek and Indian philosophies, masculine qualities include passivity or detachment, whereas in traditional Chinese philosophy, masculine qualities include being active.

This discrepancy could, of course, be explored further. Could it be that some cultures carry certain aspects of masculine energy while others carry other aspects? This would affect how "masculine" energies are defined and perceived.

My take on this is that the masculine traits common in all cultures point to this energy. In some cultures, masculine energy is emphasized from one aspect over another, pointing to an overall passive or active masculine energy. This differs from society-imposed gender roles, which would change across different cultures. I am not concerned with the "Macho Man" or the Cowboy; I am more interested in the energy that flows and is expressed as healthy, mature masculinity.

Rather than ramble on and on about my takes and opinions on this, why not explore what I feel is an excellent illustration of this all-inclusive masculine dynamic – the movie The King's Speech?

This illustration will also provide an excellent transition to dissecting the father archetype – a great platform to flesh out what this particular archetype is and the dynamics that define it.

Let's get to it.

The King's Speech Therapist (Dissecting the Father Archetype)

KING GEORGE V, PLAYED by Michael Gambon, is portrayed as a father who demands the traits of kingship from his two sons.

Colin Firth's character, who becomes King George VI, suffers from a speech impediment: constantly stutters.

In the movie, King George V yells at his son, "Get it out, boy!" to get him to stop stammering. Along comes Lionel, the speech therapist, played by Geoffrey Rush. Through Lionel, not his dad, the father archetypal energy manifested for Prince Albert.

The movie was very moving for me as I saw the two types of the father archetype being played out to bring forth genuine masculinity.

If the father archetype's role is to teach or guide the boy in how to be in the world, then King George V tried desperately to do just that with his son. He tried very hard with both sons, but his personality and how he tried to do this eventually did not allow Prince Albert to have his voice.

The first aspect of the good father archetype, as portrayed in the character of Lionel, involved setting boundaries between himself and the boy, or in this case, Prince Albert.

Even though he was an adult, Prince Albert's ego was still immature and very much identified with a boy. Prince Albert was identified as the *weakling king*, a shadow side of the king archetype, which we will discuss later.

In setting boundaries, Lionel created his kingdom or defined rules that he expected Bertie, or Prince Albert, to uphold. As Lionel declares in the movie, "My rules, my castle."

Forbidding smoking in the consulting room was one rule or boundary. Another rule was insisting on using informal names, not titles, to establish equality.

Lionel was completely willing to let go of this prestigious client to maintain these boundaries.

The father archetype, like the king archetype, which we will discuss later, sets appropriate boundaries with his children. As the father, he is the Lord of the manor.

The second thing Lionel did was to recognize Prince Albert's potential voice.

In his creativity, Lionel managed to record Bertie's voice without him being able to hear it to prove Bertie had a voice.

In other words, the speech therapist knew Bertie had a voice and could use it. He also knew that Bertie's rejection of his voice and the fear of speaking caused his impediment.

The father archetype embodies a profound ability to recognize the hidden potential within his children, in this case, the boy, and employs innovative and motivating methods to draw out that potential, facilitating its development.

With a keen perception, the father discerns the boy's unique strengths, talents, and aspirations, tailoring his approach to suit the individual. Through mentoring, guidance, and encouragement, the father creates a supportive environment that allows the boy to explore and embrace his abilities. Through challenging activities, exposure to diverse experiences, or gentle yet constructive feedback, the father empowers the boy to grow and refine his skills.

In doing so, the father instills a sense of purpose, confidence, and determination within the boy, setting him on a path of self-discovery, personal growth, and realizing his true potential.

Third, patience was extremely important in the therapeutic relationship between Lionel and Prince Albert. Bertie would throw temper tantrums and quit in frustration, like a little boy having a fit. Lionel continued to work with him despite the tantrums and the insults tossed at him.

At times, this is how it is. Children get enraged and throw fits, yet the father carries on with patience, not giving in to their anger, not taking it personally.

Again, as mentioned previously in the Greek and Hindu philosophies, masculine energy or principle is one of passivity or objectivity and not one of action, as in other cultures.

Fourth, Lionel encouraged Bertie to curse, allowing him to express a part of himself he could not exhibit under the persona of the prince and, eventually, king. Once Bertie was encouraged to use profanity, a part of him surfaced that would allow Bertie to better integrate this aspect into his true voice: the angry part, the unacceptable and rejected part.

A good father fosters an environment where his son feels safe and encouraged to express himself openly and authentically.

Recognizing that self-identity is crucial for personal growth and fulfillment, the father supports his son's journey of self-discovery. The son can confidently explore his emotions, thoughts, and passions by providing space for expression through communication, creativity, or exploration of interests.

This nurturing atmosphere allows the son to develop a strong sense of self, leading to increased self-awareness, self-esteem, and a deeper understanding of his unique identity. As a result, the son is more likely to grow into a well-adjusted, self-assured individual, ready to face life's challenges with resilience and authenticity.

This is the purpose of adolescence. Identity is being formed and created through these difficult years that form the bridge between childhood and adulthood. It is appropriate and necessary for the adolescent to explore, experiment, and even rebel.

Young Bertie was limited in doing this, so his verbal expression was negatively affected. Lionel was aware of this and encouraged Bertie's anger and use of foul language, unlocking expression and allowing Bertie's identity to evolve.

Lionel stood by Prince Albert, mentoring him and coaching him until little by little, Bertie could speak in a manner where his true voice could be heard.

Like a coach who sticks with the player until the player can coach himself, Lionel was the only one with King George VI in the recording room as he delivered a very sensitive message to the people of Great Britain and the domains of the British Empire.

The absence of criticism and name-calling was instrumental in calling forth the voice within the prince-turned-king. After this very important speech, which the prince had dreaded, he truly became King George VI. It was an initiation and ritual that needed to be wrestled with and overcome. A ritual completed alongside Lionel, the symbolic father archetype.

A key element of the movie occurred when Lionel told Bertie, "You don't have to be afraid anymore. Your father is no longer here, and you no longer have to carry him with you. It is easy to let him go."

Lionel knew that Bertie's father and brother, who both represented what being a man was to Bertie, were the ones Bertie reacted to. As a result, they blocked his voice from being heard. After Bertie was able to let them go, he was able to speak and be heard. Lionel played the good father: one who acknowledges, celebrates, mentors, coaches, and helps the boy to mature and be in the world.

The movie's end displayed the message that King George VI became the voice of inspiration for the people to motivate them through the dreadful war.

At the finale, I was moved to tears when King George VI stepped out to the balcony with his wife and two daughters, with the crowds in front of Buckingham cheering their king. Here, the archetype of the king and the masculine were very much the center for these people, who sought direction in this chaotic period.

Through this illustration, I hope I've more than outlined what the father archetype is founded on and what it projects.

Wrapping Up

I THINK HARD AND OFTEN of the men who played their part in my life, helping me to grow from the boy I was to the man I am.

I will further explore my relationships with my stepfather, uncle, and father in this work. I do this for catharsis, of allowing myself to consciously process my relationships with them and make conscious hidden emotions or memories that are trapped within.

I will also explore these relationships on behalf of the reader, who will benefit, I hope, by acknowledging their father or fathers within and without, seeing the qualities of these relationships, and unblocking any trapped energies, there are to unleash the masculine energy.

Here, I must pause and discuss the importance of unblocking emotional energies.

I have studied this concept using many different terms in psychology. However, I only recently discovered the importance of returning, feeling the emotions there, and letting them go.

I experienced this while undergoing hypnosis in a session. In my imagination, I confronted my stepfather, and I began to re-experience all the anger that I felt when I was a boy. I had to feel the anger, which then turned into tears, and only then was I able to forgive him.

After that session, I truly felt lighter and freer. I then had the amazing chance to experience the process I had studied for so long and discussed countless times with my clients.

As you read my experiences and the concepts I write about, you may have memories of the men who demonstrated mature, healthy masculine energy for you. If these memories never come, this may be an opportunity to wrestle with the pain and anger and have your catharsis.

The next chapter, which explores the king archetype, contains even more of my experiences and the king/tyrant energy in my life as a boy... my stepfather. But before we get into it, here are a few questions to help you reflect.

What is your definition of masculinity? What do you believe masculinity entails, and what traits do you associate most closely with it?

Did you grow up in the presence of your father? If so, what was your relationship with him like? Were you close, and did he motivate and guide you gently but firmly, or did he impose his will on you, even against your own will?

If you grew up with your father, what boundaries did he set in the household? How did these boundaries sit with you? Was there ever any conflict between you and him concerning the same?

Did your father foster an environment where you felt safe and encouraged to express yourself openly and authentically, or was the opposite true? Elaborate further on your answer.

Have you ever had somebody come into your life who, much like Lionel in The King's Speech, perhaps embodied the father archetype better than your father? If so, who was he, and what did he do for you?

Has this chapter perhaps brought anything else up for you?

Chapter 3: The King Archetype and the Shadow of the Tyrant – My Stepfather

Photo by William Kraus

I must admit that when commencing to write about my stepfather, I encountered a lot of resistance. Even as I now write, I find it difficult to recall memories of him and me. In psychology, this could be referred to as dissociation, where whenever you seem to forget events that happened, it usually has to do with the memory being so emotionally charged that you can't bring yourself to remember.

However, I will do my absolute best to dig into the well of my memories and to provide information and an account of things and happenings that are as accurate as possible. This book is meant for personal catharsis, to provide psychological concepts, and to genuinely help you, my dear reader. As such, I must straddle the saddle of truth as firmly as possible and do my best to lay things out as I experienced them so we can benefit as much as possible.

So, join me as I relay my past, as I remember it, with my stepfather in the picture.

Softball, Beer & Early Attempts at Straightening Me Out

AT AGE SIX OR SEVEN, I attended my stepfather's softball games, not by choice, as if they were a ritual. I didn't know it then, but they actually were.

It was a ritual for Cuban boys to share with their father in the baseball ceremony. I felt so out of place being there with my stepfather's friends. I didn't know what to think or feel.

I remember being offered beer to drink, Miller beer, as I recall. I remember the bitter taste of the beer and how disgusting it was for me. I might have spit it out, or maybe I did swallow. I quite don't recall.

At that young age, though, I decided not to be a beer drinker. Even today, as an adult, I don't drink beer, especially light beer. The feeling that I was being forced to drink beer at that early age makes me angry whenever I recall the experience.

I sensed an underlying action of "straightening" me out. The tough, macho approach to raising a boy and having him drink beer at a softball tournament appears to have been my stepfather's strategy.

As an adult, I learned that he had told my mother several times of his fear that I would turn out gay, or "maricón," and it would be her fault. I wasn't told until I was an adult that my mother would be blamed.

I think she relied on him to fix me, and I have to say that he truly did try.

Another memory was when my mother took my sisters and his two daughters, my stepsisters, shopping. It seemed to me that shopping or going to the mall was some wonderful thing that was being kept from me because I was a boy. Only the ladies went shopping, not the boys.

My mother would leave me with Mr. Tough Macho Cuban. He watched sports on the television and drank beer. I retreated to my room and played alone.

I never received any affection from him. Now, I can only guess that loving affection did not fit in with his model of being a father or of raising a real man.

Once, I was so angry with him that I went out to our apartment's balcony and began throwing his bottles of beer over the balcony. He came out and was so angry he grabbed me, hitting me repeatedly. I don't remember why I did it or even the event that led up to my behavior. I remember only that it happened.

I also remember singing and dancing in front of the bathroom mirror with a towel over my head on various occasions as if it were long hair.

He would barge into the bathroom and start hitting me with a belt. I thought, "Why? I am not doing anything wrong here, just having fun."

Another time, he entered the bathroom while I was trying on my sister's skirt. Again, the anger on his face and the belting I received for playing caused me to think, "Why? What is wrong with pretending?"

The thoughts these events triggered created the belief that I could not just 'be' as a boy. Only girls were allowed to 'be'.

My sisters weren't scolded or hit because they spoke with their hands or because their intonations sounded a certain way.

On the other hand, as a boy, I had to fit into the mold of what boys looked like. I felt repressed as a child and envied my sisters because they could just be themselves.

They enjoyed beautiful things. They didn't do difficult physical tasks, like throwing out the garbage or mowing the lawn.

Being a girl had great advantages in my family.

As an adult, I now understand why my stepfather attempted to mold me a certain way. In the seventies in Miami, a city mixed with Southern and Cuban cultures, both of which emphasized that tough macho man-image, it would have been a disservice just to allow me to behave in an effeminate way that I was behaving. I heard the same message at school from the other boys that I heard at home, "Don't act like that; that is not how boys act, and you are a boy!"

Thank God we live in a different society today, and Miami as a city has evolved. However, back then, that is how things were. The fear my mother had with me, as well as my stepfather's repulsion towards my effeminate behavior, is understandable: not acceptable, but certainly understandable.

And this particular bit of my backstory brings us to the king archetype. I'll explore the salient elements of the king archetype and try to tie them into my life's examples and happenings.

The King Archetype – A Dissection

THE ARCHETYPE OF THE king deals with two facets, according to Moore and Gillette. These two facets are the creation of order and fertility and blessing.

My stepfather attempted to create order in his house and his kingdom, and this ordering was based on conventional societal norms, and my behavior was not in line. The challenge comes with how the king will create order. This is the challenge the king faces. Will he be a fair and just king, or will he become a tyrant?

The archetype of the king has a shadow side, with both active and passive poles. The active pole is called the tyrant. This archetype can, for instance, be observed in the stories of King Herod in the Christian tradition and with King Saul from the Jewish tradition. Both Herod and Saul became identified with the position of the king, minus the positive archetypal energy which no longer manifested through them.

In the story of King Herod, the archetypal energy of the king was to be embodied in the baby Christ who was born. In the case of King Saul, the prophet Samuel had informed him that David was to be the new king, and he needed to step down. The fear of being usurped is part of the tyrant's archetypal energy.

Similar dynamics to those witnessed in the King Saul and King Herod examples are present in nuclear households, as far as the masculine archetype goes. Let's delve some more into this...

The father doesn't want to give up his role as head of the family and, like Herod, destroys or kills off the new energy that arises in his children. His children's creativity, or way of being, becomes a threat if his values and beliefs are not revered or honored.

I'll use my example as an illustration:

My way of being was new to my stepfather, and it was intolerable for him to accept. It touched upon his homophobia, and this was very difficult for him. In his realm, he would not have a gay child present. His kingdom made no room for someone different, like me.

Let's look at some examples of similar dynamics in modern history that you may be familiar with.

Examples of the Tyrant King Archetype in Modern History

A PERFECT ILLUSTRATION of the tyrant king archetype from modern history would be the case of Adolf Hitler.

Hitler's pursuit of creating an Aryan race was driven by a desire for a homogenous society under strict norms, where anyone perceived as different or divergent from the established order would be excluded or forcibly sterilized. This vision of a "kingdom" ruled by the shadow king, the tyrant, led to brutal measures against those who did not conform. Any attempts to correct what he saw as deviancy within the kingdom were met with extreme actions, culminating in the horrific motivation for genocide. The Holocaust, a dark chapter in history, exemplifies the horrible consequences of such ideologies, where millions of innocent lives were systematically exterminated to eliminate those deemed undesirable or a threat to the imposed order.

Hitler's ideology was grounded in an extremist version of nationalism and racial purity, driven by a twisted belief in superiority and dominance. His regime utilized propaganda, fear, and the manipulation of public opinion to gain support for their brutal policies. It led to a reign of terror and persecution of various groups, particularly Jews, Romani people, disabled individuals, homosexuals, and others considered "undesirable." This ruthless quest for conformity and control ultimately resulted in unimaginable suffering and loss, a stark reminder of the dangers of unchecked power and the importance of upholding the principles of inclusivity, tolerance, and respect for diversity in any society.

Authoritarian or totalitarian societies, especially those of decades past and those we are currently dealing with, are also great illustrations of the same.

In these societies, the indoctrination of children starts at an early age, as they are taught the regime's principles. Through repetitive activities like singing or chanting phrases in school, these ideologies become deeply ingrained in their minds. Neuroscientists have observed that this process leads to the formation of neuronal networks in the brain. These networks of neurons contain repeated thoughts and behaviors. They are sealed by emotions associated with indoctrination, found in totalitarian or authoritarian societies, making the memories much more enduring.

As young minds continuously recite the party's philosophy, their thinking becomes impaired due to the overwhelming influence of the leading ideology being pushed down on them.

The use of repetitive practices is a powerful tool in shaping the beliefs and behaviors of the younger generation, as their developing brains are highly receptive to such conditioning.

By instilling the regime's ideas early, these societies aim to create a collective mindset that aligns with the party's goals, effectively suppressing independent thought and critical reasoning. Therefore, the noted Intelligencia of a country is the antithesis of this. This process of indoctrination not only affects children's creative and independent abilities but impacts their emotional and social development, as they become more inclined to conform to the established ideology rather than exploring alternative perspectives.

As a result, the authoritarian regime maintains a tight grip on society, ensuring loyalty and obedience, but at the cost of stifling individual independence and creativity.

I see this first-hand with my partner, himself a product of communist Cuba.

As an adult and one with very high liberal democratic and capitalist ideals, he is still able to recite all the songs and phrases of the Communist Party that were taught to him as a child. He remembers the lines and words very clearly and gets emotional when he sings or recites them. This also tends to trigger a reaction in me since I had no experience of this, being born in Miami. When he sings his childhood anthem, it seems as if all the anger my family and fellow Cuban exiles in Miami had and have come rushing in, and I strongly feel them.

Even though he is not a Communist, the system has been able to penetrate his psyche and create strong neuronal networks that persist until the present day. These techniques, clearly part of the tyrant side of the king archetype, have been used by all systems and governments that side with this archetypal energy.

Let's now get back to my own story, featuring the tyrant king who was my stepfather and how I saw my very first adult movie as a pre-pubescent boy, against my will.

Another Attempt to Straighten Me Out- A Belt, A Chair, & 'Straight' Porn

I CLEARLY REMEMBER one day when, as a child, I was taken by my stepfather to his friend's house. My stepfather's friend, the owner of a large cement company and a very wealthy man. His house was a ranch-style house in the then outskirts of South Florida in the community of Miramar, affluent at the time. He owned a large property with a pool and a tennis court. I think it was a day of playing baseball, so the event must have been on a Sunday. We went to Paul's house, and no one else was there, only the "good old boys" of the baseball club. I was the only child present.

The men gathered outside in the pool and began drinking beer while they swam. For whatever reason, I don't recall, I was taken to the living room and tied with a belt to a chair. It could very well be this was done so that I wouldn't fall in the pool and drown. OK, providing the benefit of the doubt here, but maybe not.

Who knows?

I was facing a television, and on it was a porn movie. I remember not knowing what I was looking at on the T.V. I still don't recall exactly, but I do know that I was not supposed to be watching that sort of movie. I recall feeling I was watching something bad when my step-granduncle came in and was surprised to find me watching the film. He reacted, corroborating what I had thought- that it was a bad movie, and he then untied me. He asked my stepfather what I was doing watching that type of movie. My stepfather said that the movie would do me good. I was angry then, and only the years have cooled my rage. Upon arriving home, I told my mother what had happened, which in turn caused another argument.

Years later, my mother and I recently had a conversation, and this event came up. My mother doesn't recall me ever telling her of this. She asked while sobbing, what kind of a mother would have allowed this? She asked for forgiveness. I replied that I no longer hold these feelings and that she did nothing wrong, only to allow herself to marry this man. The tyrant energy affects many.

Drawing from my example above, the tyrant resorts to attempting to change innate behaviors or identities to enforce conformity. By targeting deeply rooted aspects of a person's nature or identity, the tyrant seeks to mold them into compliant subjects who unquestioningly follow his imposed norms. This approach often involves suppressing one's individuality and denying personal agency, as the tyrant aims to shape those under him according to his agenda.

Back to my story...

At the age of ten, when my mother finally had enough of our tyrant and told him to leave, I recall feeling divided. I went to my room, threw myself on my bed, and cried. I was sad to see my stepfather go. Then, in my crying, I also recall that a small sense of joy and peace bubbled up. The battle was over; I was safe now. I now believe my crying was due to losing a father figure. I believed I was losing the king; I needed to grow up and face the world.

Even though this man was not good to me and presented the shadow oppressive side of the king archetype, it was better to have this type of king than no king at all. I think this is similar to the Iraqi people losing their dictator. The same sense is felt among the people whenever a dictator is overthrown. The tyrant king can at least maintain order and structure, even if he is unjust and unfair. Without a king, the energies of chaos enter the kingdom and threaten annihilation.

Let's look at an example that you may be well familiar with.

When the Americans overthrew Saddam Hussein, the news media created the image of dancing in the streets and twenty-four hours of partying. But recently, I learned that many mainstream and independent news organizations, like the BBC and Associated Press correspondents, noticed that only a small group were partying. The loss of their king was frightening for many in Iraqi society.

Again, the tyrant was gone. However, this tyrant was clever and governed with an iron fist to keep out the chaotic energies of the extremist Islamic movements to the east and the fragments of warlords in the north.

Tyrants rule by fear, which is how they maintain their kingdoms intact. "If we don't do this or give up that, chaos will occur!" This is standard speech in the land of the tyrant.

To maintain the status quo and keep things homogenous or "united," a tighter grip on society is needed. Diversity is too threatening to the tyrant archetype.

This was especially true with my stepdad.

In my childhood home, I was too diverse. My stepfather instilled fear in my mother by telling her how horrible things would be if she allowed me to be a fag. She bought into that thinking, and, in her fear, she allowed him to unleash everything he thought would deter me from being the homosexual man I am today. The chaotic energy of the unknown is frightening. That is why so many remain in the land of the tyrant, to avoid the sea serpents at the end of the ocean.

But even as horrible and emotionless as my relationship with my stepdad was, there was a silver lining to our dark cloud, and we had something in common. An appreciation for art.

An Affinity for Art– The One Thing We Had in Common

I WOULD WAKE UP EARLY on Saturdays and accompany my stepfather to his business. To my surprise, my stepfather's company dealt with silk-screen art, a type of graphic art still used today.

I found it fascinating to be in this warehouse where there were so many colors of paint. Being an innate artist, I enjoyed working with him on those Saturday mornings.

Seeing my step-uncle, who also worked there, pouring the paint onto the silk canvas, I watched him spread the various colors over the silk until the image surfaced in the many colors used. I remembered the graphic letterings of an airline, and I thought, "How wonderful" to create those posters or signature branding.

As I write this, I am quite surprised that in writing about the man who I always thought helped make my childhood a nightmare, I now realize that we share one thing in common: we were both artists. It seems we were both moved by the aesthetics of things. Even though his work was mostly used for advertising and was very structured, it was creative and artistic nevertheless.

Allow me to digress... we'll get back to my stepdad's silk-screen art in a bit. I need to touch on a cultural aspect quickly, which I'll tie into the subject.

I understand that my stepfather lost an opportunity to get to know and have a relationship with me. I was his first son-though "step." He had daughters from a previous marriage but not a son, so I was his firstborn male in many respects.

At other times in history, the firstborn male was important in the family. The firstborn male was the benefactor of the family business and learned the secrets from the father that had been handed to him from his father before him. This was a wonderful chance for him to teach me. I could have admired him. I could have tried to follow and model him rather than hate him.

Instead of teaching me about silk-screening and understanding his world, which would have excited me, he yelled at me to sweep the factory floor and keep the paint cans in order. In writing this, I get emotional, feeling sadness and anger.

I was just a little boy trying to understand the men around me. I longed to be taught and taken under men's wing so that one day, I could truly be one. This was difficult when the man closest to me rejected me. Maybe it was that I was not his blood but a son only through his marriage. Maybe it was indeed that me being gay was not an option for him. I will never truly know. What I write is only my perception, so I think it is important.

The perception of a boy regarding how the significant men in the boy's life are captured plays a vital role in how the boy is to develop healthy masculinity. In this way, the masculine archetypes of the proper king may flow through the life of the boy-turned-man.

When I read this section to my partner Jose, he made an interesting observation. Jose is similar to my youngest brother. Both were the youngest among their siblings, raised by their biological fathers. Jose's father was a stepfather to Jose's older brothers.

My partner pointed out that if my stepfather had taken the time to teach me, to model for me, and to initiate me into the world of men, my relationship with my stepfather could have been similar to Jose's two older brothers' relationship with his dad.

They admire him truly and treat him as the father he was to them. In this view of things, I pondered that my stepfather channeled the energy of the tyrant archetype, and Jose's father allowed for a more authentic Kingship energy to come through.

With this off my chest, I'd now like to touch upon an intriguing concept – the transference concept.

The Transference Concept

WAY TOO MANY MEN TODAY have not had good relationships with their fathers, whether biological or fathers, through marriage, as in my case.

These poor relationships, whether characterized by tyranny or absenteeism, whether physically or emotionally harmful, leave the boy where he is: a boy. Without the ritual or initiation, men are only men in physical and chronological terms. Their psyches are very much in the boy realm, leaving them immature.

For better illustration, I'll draw on examples I see in my clinical practice.

In my practice, I see various men with different presenting complaints. I can see that they are psychological boys at the root, sitting in front of me with the unconscious hope that I would be the father they never had.

In the depth psychology schools, this is known as *transference*.

Suppose I can hold the father image for them and be the father they did not have. In that case, through the work of analysis, it is hopeful that they are finally initiated into manhood, and away from the immature boyhood stage they're stuck in.

Let's take the example of one of my clients. We'll call him Jay.

Jay is a very successful professional. And I mean very, very successful. But while he's strong and assertive and an exceptionally confident leader in his profession, he has perpetually struggled with his intimate relationships with women.

In his current relationship, for example, he struggles to either keep the guard low in an attempt to relate, thus allowing for abuse and being taken advantage of, or build a thick wall, emotionally isolating himself and keeping his abusive girlfriend out. Either way, his relationship was not healthy. This supremely successful professional man is a mere boy afraid of relating healthily to the feminine.

Understanding a healthy masculine stance requires the appropriate assertiveness to set up and maintain boundaries. Boundaries are a staple element with the king archetype.

By being assertive, the man can effectively communicate his needs and limits with respect, fostering respect for himself and his partner/others. As an archetype, the king exemplifies the wise and benevolent ruler who governs with firm yet compassionate authority. In the same way, embracing this aspect of masculinity entails taking responsibility for your actions, making informed decisions, and protecting both personal integrity and the well-being of those within your sphere of influence.

By mastering the art of assertiveness and boundary-setting, you can navigate life with grace, strength, and fairness, embodying the noble qualities associated with the king archetype.

Back to my client, if he would be better able to connect with his inner king archetypal energy, he could then confront his girlfriend appropriately, letting her know what he feels comfortable doing in their relationship and what makes him uncomfortable. In this case, the obvious passivity in my client produces such tremendous tension in the unconscious that, like a pressure cooker, the result is an explosive outburst that could lead quite easily to verbal and physical aggression towards his girlfriend.

Like many men, my client did not have a father figure present during his childhood to model or teach him about healthy boundaries or being a king over his kingdom.

Let's examine another one of my clients. We'll call him Woody.

Woody is often confused about whether to allow himself to love a woman he is dating or to indulge in the many rationalizations of why he should end it. Being rational, he can develop the most sophisticated lists of pros and cons that would ultimately confuse anyone, including himself.

When we probe deeper into his emotional world, his fear is so intense that I feel I am with a boy, leading him by his hand to come with me while he locks his feet, crying that he is afraid. I must listen, help him organize his thoughts about his feelings, and nudge him to apply his insights in behavioral ways. Being a father involves allowing the boy to express his fears and emotions while being stable, firmly guiding his son through the fear into action.

Finally, there's Ray, a gay male client raised in a home where the father was stoic and logical and the mother emotionally labile.

Ray's emotional struggle revolves around a complex interplay between sensitivity, insecurity, and controlling behavior within his relationship. He is torn between his desire for love and affection and his fear of vulnerability and potential pain. This inner conflict leads him to act out in a controlling manner towards his partner as a misguided way of maintaining a sense of power and avoiding emotional exposure.

The therapeutic work for Ray involves, among other things, embracing and acknowledging his strong emotions and longing for romance while learning to establish healthy emotional boundaries. By developing the ability to contain and process his feelings internally, he can help foster a more balanced and fulfilling connection with his partner.

The King Archetype & the Need for "Permeable" Rules and Boundaries

WHEN TAPPING INTO THE king archetype energy, appropriate boundaries must be part and parcel.

It is important to understand the kingdom as your inner world and learn how to contain and protect it. And like a healthy kingdom, we must allow for some permeability.

What do we mean by this?

Take the example of a literal kingdom/country. There must be a flexible boundary where the citizenry may travel freely, and visitors from other lands may enter for tourism. Trade must flow, allowing for imports and exports to stabilize the economy. Similarly, proper attention to your inner world is just as important as a head of a country focusing on domestic issues. We can't always focus on the outer world, just like we can't always entertain all foreign policy.

For Ray, for instance, if I can hold the father's energy, I hope to help him reflect on his emotional needs and help him verbalize his needs to his partner. This, in turn, allows for a healthy dialogue that maintains a strong connection in their relationship.

Moving on Beyond the Experience of Having Lived

with a Tyrant

IF YOU HAD THE UNFORTUNATE childhood experience of not having a proper father figure or having lived with a tyrant, please understand that it is essential that you move beyond that experience so that you can channel the healthier masculine archetype.

Having grown up without a positive father figure or having lived with a tyrant as a father can deeply impact your perception of masculinity and influence your behavior and relationships as an adult. The absence of a nurturing and supportive father can lead to feelings of abandonment, low self-esteem, and difficulties in forming healthy connections. Similarly, living with an authoritarian father figure can create a sense of fear, powerlessness, and emotional wounds that linger into adulthood.

To overcome these challenges and cultivate a healthier masculine archetype, you must confront and process your childhood experiences. Analytic sessions, such as therapy or counseling, provide a safe and supportive environment for this healing process. In therapy, you can explore your emotions, beliefs, and behavioral patterns stemming from your early experiences. By delving into these past wounds, you can gain insights into how your upbringing has shaped your understanding of masculinity and relationships. And the emotions that you feel and confront will open the gates to allow the masculine energy to begin flowing.

Here's how an analytic session with an astrologist I admire went:

In my session, I was taken back to my childhood through hypnosis, or as some call it, deep visualization. In my mind, I went back to the warehouse where Jessy, my stepfather, had his workshop. I was back in the room where the paints were neatly stacked, and the darkroom held the photographic prints that would be transferred to the silk for printing.

It is there where I went to see my stepfather. I saw his face, his angry, stern face. Very rarely did he smile at me or laugh, only when he was being sinister. I went there, and I told him:

"Jessy, I wish you could have known me better, and I you. I really needed you. I tried to get you to like me, but it seemed you were always mad at me. Whenever I tried to sing, act, dance, or be myself, you got angrier and often hit me or said

terrible things. I am here now, Jessy. I loved you as my second dad, Papi. Now I realize that possibly your fear kept you from accepting me."

"Quite possibly, you did not know how to handle or treat me, which resulted in your insults and aggression. I know you wanted a son, and if you treated me as your son by accepting my whole being, you thought it might result in a big mistake, putting me in danger. With tough love, you truly believed you could make me a man so that I could survive in the world. With your anger, you thought I would be initiated. I allow the possibility that you wanted the best for me but didn't know how to give it to me. I forgive you."

And just like that, I finally was able to forgive. Certainly, I still get quite emotional when I reflect on my experiences with him, and I get sad and enraged. Still, the analytic sessions have helped me arrive at a point where, despite my emotions, I can forgive and move forward.

Let's reflect before we move on to the next archetype:

How did your father demonstrate his "king masculine archetype energy" while you were growing up, and how did it impact your relationship with him?

Can you recall specific instances of boundaries your father set for you during your childhood? How did these boundaries shape your development and sense of responsibility?

Reflecting on your father's role as the "king" in your household, do you believe he was fair in his decisions and actions? Can you give examples that support your perspective?

Were there moments when you felt your father exhibited more tyrannical traits than a positive "king" archetype? How did these instances affect your feelings and experiences within the family?

Looking back, what aspects of your father's approach as the household "king" do you wish he had done differently? How would those changes have influenced your upbringing and relationship with him?

Finally, did you grow up without a father figure, or perhaps a father who was a flat-out tyrant at home? What are some issues that you grapple with to this day because of it?

As you reflect further, is there anything you want to add regarding the contents of this chapter? It could be memories evoked, realizations made, etc.

Chapter 4: The Magician Archetype:-My Uncle

MY UNCLE ALWAYS REPRESENTED another time and another place for me, especially when compared to the unsavory experience I had growing up with my stepfather.

In my opinion, he is akin to the main character of the 1950s television series, "Father Knows Best."

Like the character, he possesses an inherent wisdom and a sense of authority that exudes a comforting and reassuring presence. His guidance and advice are highly regarded by family and friends alike, often sought after in times of uncertainty.

Much like the fictional character, he navigates through life's challenges with a blend of firmness and compassion, always striving to make the best decisions for the well-being of those around him. His demeanor reflects a time-honored belief in traditional family values, maintaining a genuine interest in the lives of his loved ones while offering unwavering support and encouragement.

Despite the evolving times, my uncle's timeless qualities of kindness, understanding, and a genuine desire to see others thrive make him a treasured figure, reminiscent of the beloved father figure from a bygone era.

But allow me to track back and begin at the beginning.

My Uncle's House – A Vastly Different Kingdom

MY EARLIEST MEMORIES of my uncle take me back to a time when I was sent to be with my cousins in an effort to have me lose weight and be surrounded by boys rather than my sisters at home.

My mother had this unscientific theory that boys will not develop into men if they aren't thin when they reach puberty. Their penises will remain small and be trapped in a boy's body.

I still have not discovered where that maternal theory came from. I thought it was cultural; however, when I asked other Cubans, they all gave me a puzzled look and told me they'd never heard of such a thing.

However, in all her "medical" wisdom and wanting the best for me as every mother does, my mom sent me away to my uncle's place for the first time when I was ten.

Arriving at my uncle's place on that summer day, I recall the drive up a gravel road leading to a wooden house structure in the mountains. The property was forested, and I felt I had traveled to my first international destination. I had never seen tall trees or the land go so high to form those Virginia mountains.

Needless to say, after the description I have already given of my uncle, his kingdom was very different from my stepfather's and my home and upbringing.

In his kingdom, the citizens went to a different church, the Seventh-Day Adventist Church, and ate very different foods, being themselves vegetarian, and the day was structured very differently from the manner to which I was accustomed.

For starters, breakfast was eaten as if it were dinner, with the typical foods found in dinner: rice, beans, and a substitute meat. Lunch was pretty usual, sandwiches and the like, and then dinner was like breakfast with granola or some other light entree.

We were awoken early, around 6 a.m., and my cousins and I had to do the daily chores before breakfast. The bedroom had to be cleaned and organized, and we had other house duties. A list on the fridge stated who was responsible for what.

The climax of the week was the Sabbath or Saturday. We didn't do chores that day, and it was like a wonderful holiday. We'd wake up, get dressed in our best, and go to church to hear my uncle, the church minister, preach. I was introduced as the cousin from Miami to all those Southern folks. I enjoyed being popular there in that small Virginian church. I remember admiring my uncle as he addressed the crowds, and I thought he was the best pastor ever. I was so proud of him.

My uncle was my version of the idealized father. I could never find fault as a boy growing up with him. My deep-seated fantasy was, "Why hadn't my uncle married my mother?"

Of course, I had no understanding of what incest was all about, yet in my mind, I expressed my projection of the ideal mother and father and how I needed them.

The Magician Archetype

MY UNCLE COULD TRANSFORM and change my life into something magical and special. I had gone into another dimension of reality when I spent this and other summers with him and his family.

Things like the house had no television, and the family custom of listening to "Story Hour" on the radio in the afternoon was as if life had taken me back to a different period.

Because of this transformative effect, my uncle represented the masculine archetype of the magician.

The magician archetype embodies profound awareness, keen insight, and the presence of the observing ego within their mindset and psyche. This archetype represents the capacity to perceive the hidden truths and deeper meanings behind life's experiences, empowering you to see beyond the surface and delve into the mysteries of existence.

The magician's mastery lies in their ability to navigate the realms of consciousness, utilizing their intuitive minds to understand the interconnectedness of all things. Like a skillful alchemist, the magician can transform challenges into opportunities for growth and transformation, tapping into their inner wisdom to find creative solutions.

By embodying the observing ego, the magician can detach from personal biases and emotions, allowing them to view situations objectively and accurately. Through their awareness and insight, the magician archetype inspires others to awaken their inner wisdom and harness the power of conscious transformation.

Back to my uncle and my experiences with him...

My first summer with my uncle represented a turning point in my life in the spirit of this view of the magician archetype.

Growing up under a strong mother and sisters, the genuine man was mostly kept from me consciously. I had my mother as a positive mother figure and my stepfather as a negative manifestation of the tyrant.

My uncle, though, sparked in me a positive fatherly image. He also seemed just, compassionate, and able to guide me.

The story of Merlin comes to mind here.

Young Arthur needed instruction and guidance to develop the skills and character to become the king. Merlin guided Arthur to self-contain his inner forces for his good. If young Arthur had not learned to properly channel his inner strength and impulses, then immaturity and failure would have been his fate, and the mature masculine archetype of the king would have never emerged.

A young boy needs to look up to a father figure and feel proud of who his father is. Many men have chosen professions out of their pride for their fathers.

The father can spark the young boy's desire to commence the path to fulfilling his destiny.

And this was no different for me.

Sitting in the pews in a small church in Virginia, I saw my uncle light up with passion and spirit, delivering a message of hope and guidance to his church members.

I focused on how he talked and moved around the pulpit. This sense of awe and pride sparked a desire in me to lead and inspire others. I felt that I could follow my uncle one day, and he would be proud of me.

In writing this, I am moved and get emotional. Truly, it is a powerful thing to have a man stir the inner strivings of a young boy.

My uncle made my manhood and sense of purpose conscious. The magician archetype aims to make known what is less obvious and subtle in one's life.

Transforming and Thriving in the "Land of Boys"

AT TEN YEARS OLD, I had no consciousness of my boyhood. I only remember thinking how unfair it was that I was not a girl so that I could enjoy what my sisters enjoyed.

My sisters seemed to have all the fun.

They went shopping, got to wear long dresses and makeup, and spent much time with my mother. My sisters seemed to rule the house, with the men, mere servants, attending them as if they were ladies in waiting.

As a boy, I hated doing the "boy" things, like throwing out the trash, mowing the lawn, lifting heavy things, bringing in the groceries, etc.

Being with my uncle and my cousins in that southwest Virginian countryside kingdom, I saw that the boys ruled. My aunt was the only feminine energy present at the time. It felt good being with my male cousins. I felt included and loved in a healthy manner.

Before the age of ten, I had only a few male friends. I remember Albert and Mark. But that was all. Other than with them, I felt comfortable with girls and afraid of boys to some extent. It was not until living with my uncle that summer that my boyhood was awakened and made conscious.

In my uncle's kingdom, the boy could "come out" and be free and happy. Being a boy felt good for once.

But let me track back for a bit before I get ahead of myself here...

I was pretty overweight when I went up on my first visit with my uncle and his family.

I was told by my mother and an Asian doctor she visited that I would fail to develop as a man if I continued on the path I was going. I was prescribed hormones, and my mother was warned that I needed to be placed on a diet.

Even though I do not recall the doctor telling my mother these specific details, I captured this warning intuitively from the short phrases my mother uttered during family conversations. I had not felt good about being a boy and was often told that I was "defective" in many ways.

Now, in my uncle's kingdom, being healthy was an undercurrent philosophy that permeated everyday life:

Vegetarianism was the norm, and running and playing outside in the healthy air of the countryside were all part of this summer vacation. Little did I know that I would transform myself there.

I lost weight and felt alive with my cousins. I was exposed to a world where the flies lit up at night, and the land rose and fell, contrary to the flatness of South Florida. Those days of my childhood were like something out of Huckleberry Finn, and I roamed with my cousins through a rustic paradise complete with creeks, bugs, snakes, and endless mysteries to explore.

That was the land of boys, and it was there that I began to flourish and grow.

And this brings us to an important aspect of the magician archetype:

The masculine archetype of the magician serves as a powerful catalyst, enabling us to delve deep within ourselves and bring our inherent qualities and potential to the surface.

Reflecting on personal experience, I possessed all the fundamental traits necessary for becoming a man during my boyhood. However, I could not fully embrace and embody these attributes due to limited access or understanding of them. The magician archetype thus symbolizes the transformative journey, granting the capacity to unlock hidden aspects of yourself, ultimately facilitating the realization of true masculinity by tapping into the wellspring of innate abilities and virtues lying dormant within.

In being with my male cousins and my uncle that summer, the masculine energy summoned the boy inside of me to grow and develop. My boyhood was sickly unhealthy, and I needed other boys and men. Going to be with my uncle that summer was very important to my survival as a healthy boy and, in turn, my development into a healthy man.

The experience also reflects a characteristic of the magician archetype: *delving into the depths of my psyche to reconnect with the powerful forces that shape one's identity and development.*

Witnessing my uncle in his role as a pastor, I recognized the latent leadership qualities within myself. I did not view my uncle as a tyrant, which was unusual. In the past, my exposure to authority figures had been marred by experiences of tyranny and abuse, shaping my perception of leadership. However, my uncle exemplified a different kind of leader who governed with empathy and wisdom. His compassionate and discerning approach shattered those preconceived notions. His leadership style felt genuine and authentic, instilling a sense of respect and admiration. It opened my eyes to the possibility of leadership that could inspire and uplift rather than intimidate and oppress.

Through observing my uncle's leadership, I began to envision myself as a leader capable of fostering positive change. His example showed me that leadership could be about serving others, making a difference, and creating a nurturing environment where people could thrive. This newfound perspective sparked a desire to grow into a leader who could positively influence the lives of others, just as my uncle had done for me.

His impact on my perception of leadership remains a guiding force in my journey toward becoming a leader who leads with compassion, understanding, and a genuine concern for the well-being of those I may someday have the privilege to lead.

The Magician's 20-Minute Rule & His Key to Unlock the King Within

BACK TO MY STORY...

I recall a summer day sitting at a pew in that small Virginia church and the hymns being sung by the congregation. After the last hymn before the sermon, my stomach filled with excitement. I knew now that the star of the show was about to make his entrance.

My uncle sat in the large middle chair right behind the pulpit. That chair was reserved for the one who was honored to give the sermon. My uncle stood up, faced the people, and began his eloquent speech. He had a rule of speaking no longer than twenty minutes. He believed that for twenty minutes, people could stay focused and listen. After that, people's minds shut down, and you have lost them.

I have also stayed with that rule for my speeches ever since.

When my uncle got up and spoke, he allowed something deep within him to transform him into a channel or vessel. The audience was caught up in a trance or spell. I do not think my uncle would regard himself as a sorcerer, but in how he spoke, that is what he became.

His words were inspiring and touching. He would give a call to action, and people would heed. He was very moving, and I knew I wanted to be like him.

My uncle had the key to unlock a part of my potential. Through my admiration of him, a part of me was already so much like him; that part resonated and woke me up that summer of 1981. Like Merlin, my uncle's influence managed to awaken the inner king within me, urging me to step forward and seize my rightful place, like pulling the sword from the stone and claiming my kingdom. Alongside this transformation, another part of me was stirred—the monk inside. This newfound awareness connected me to a sense of spirituality and introspection as if an ancient calling guided me toward contemplation and inner growth.

My uncle's guidance and inspiration empowered me to embrace my potential as a leader and spiritual seeker. His influence awakened my personality's assertive and reflective aspects, merging the qualities within me of a king and monk. This harmonious combination set me on a profound journey of self-discovery that would continue to shape my identity and purpose as I ventured into the world with newfound strength and purpose.

As a child, I always had the small flame of spirituality and all things religious. I was very sensitive in capturing the deep messages that arose from within about life and the divine. I did not know exactly what it all meant, and to this day, I still have the same messages flowing up from my inner depths.

Raised as a Roman Catholic, I admired the men who walked around in their long black robes and cassocks. There was something mysterious about the way they lived their lives. Being in churches and cathedrals was like coming home for me, and at the same time, I looked around in awe and wonder. Stained glass windows took me to a place where I could feel alive and in total ecstasy. I was, and still am, deeply moved by the numinous.

But what touched me the most were the rituals my uncle observed:

Every morning after breakfast, he and my aunt and cousins gathered in the living room. My aunt would open a book of daily readings and read the story for the day. She read very well, and her intonation captured me and took me to wherever the story was based. After the reading, we would sing a couple of songs about how our sins were washed away or how we were Christian Soldiers. I had never experienced that family time before and found it so wonderful and intimate. It was as if I was witnessing the Holy Family right before my eyes.

In those morning devotions, the symbol of family was there. If I did not know better, I would have thought I was on the set of some 1950s television show. The wholesomeness and joy of these morning and evening gatherings were like I had discovered a treasure. Here, again, is the magician's work, the transformation and enchantment at work.

Due to my sensitive spiritual nature, I blossomed during those summers. It was no wonder I decided at eleven to become baptized into their faith and tradition and become a Seventh-Day Adventist. I wanted to be a part of that holy family as I perceived them. Of course, that caused many conflicts back in the land of the tyrant once I returned to the Magic City, but it was worth it.

It gave me the strength to begin the separation a boy needs from his mother and the world she represents and set on his journey to truly becoming a man.

Initiation

IN CERTAIN TRADITIONAL tribes and communities, a significant rite of passage exists for young boys to transition into manhood. This initiatory process, deeply rooted in cultural and spiritual beliefs, holds immense significance as it marks the boys' transformation from childhood to adulthood. Typically overseen by elders or spiritual leaders, the initiates undergo tests, challenges, and teachings designed to instill vital values, skills, and responsibilities required of men within their tribe.

These rituals strengthen their connection to their cultural heritage, foster camaraderie among peers, and impart essential knowledge for their roles as future leaders, protectors, and contributors to the community's well-being.

By completing this initiatory journey, these young men earn the respect and recognition of their tribe, becoming integral members entrusted with preserving their traditions and ensuring the continuity of their unique way of life.

Onto my initiatory process...

The conflicts I went through concerning my change of denomination were the beginning of my initiatory passage. I would even say it lasted into my early twenties. It was my uncle who manifested the magician energy, and it was he who was essential in my commencing my initiation.

I was baptized around the age of twelve, and from then on, I had agreed to accept the standards that this new church upheld. They were indeed strict: no dancing, no wearing of jewelry, and no going to the movies. I agreed to uphold these, and I did a very good job in doing so.

In my mind, I was on a path, and I was determined to follow it.

I could look straight into the future and see my uncle as my final destination, as the man I now chose to be. In serving as a male role model, my uncle was powerful.

Allow me to speak a little more about modeling as a whole:

Modeling is an important element in the process of learning as well as for psychological development. In today's society, I often see the unspoken message of "Do what I say, not what I do." We see how business and financial ethics have gone out the window.

Let's take the example of our banks and mega companies:

The corruption in our banks and corporations is evident when common folks are expected to pay back what was lent to them when the banks and corporations themselves are quickly released from their debt through bankruptcy law. Unfortunately, it's the hypocrisy of the absolute highest order, and modeling is a concept that has been nearly decimated in today's world. And we are all the worse for it.

Let's examine a study conducted on monkeys as we glean more about the modeling concept. I'll keep the study example concise and simplify the terminologies used so we can quickly get a grasp on the findings and move on with our story:

In a research study conducted by Subiaul and colleagues in 2004, they observed that monkeys don't imitate new physical actions they witness, like copying movements or gestures made by others (motor imitation). However, the study revealed that monkeys can mimic novel cognitive processes, which means they can copy new ways of thinking or problem-solving strategies (cognitive imitation). This suggests that while monkeys may not replicate physical actions, they can learn from each other's mental approaches, indicating a form of social learning based on cognitive skills rather than direct motor imitation.

Based on the study's results, it seems that the brain organizes the copying of non-actions/non-words in a specific way. First, when we observe something, we turn it into a rule in our mind (cognitive imitation). Then, if it's about copying actions or words, we create a program in our brain to follow and do what we observe (motor or vocal imitation).

When someone says one thing but does something different, we immediately notice the difference. Our brain stores the unspoken or acted-out rule that represents what happens.

Going by this study, we, like the monkeys, are not just robotically copying others' emotions or behaviors.

We observe and interpret, creating rules that we then imitate. Even though the study does not mention this, it is my interpretation that we observe and make interpretations based on various factors like the tone or mood, the message being communicated, and our inner emotional response to what we observe. Yes, it is complex and incredible.

Once these factors come together, we act out or imitate the action and the attitude and mood that went with the original action we observed.

Therefore, the magician energy is one where this type of modeling is reinforced and used...

Returning to Merlin's story, in the mythic Arthurian stories, Merlin teaches young Arthur many skills and, more importantly, the hidden messages underlying these skills. These messages behind the ordinary, mundane skills bind to a deeper layer of Arthur's mind or psyche; those lessons then take root and grow as trees within.

The magician archetype, therefore, is an energy that takes us from simply performing mundane skills to the more profound message encoded in the actions.

You can see yet another all-too-clear example in the movie 'The Karate Kid."

In the movie Karate Kid, Miyagi, the wise old karate teacher, takes Daniel, the dark-haired Italian Jersey boy, under his wing and guides the boy into becoming a man.

He does this by making Daniel do the seemingly stupid task of waxing a car. As I watched this movie as a teenager, I remember thinking that Miyagi was simply taking advantage of Daniel just to get his car shined.

But it was through these mundane tasks that Miyagi could teach Daniel the important hand movements to defend himself later. Children, especially young boys, need to learn specific tasks, which, however mundane, are essential for the life lessons they will encounter.

Another movie depicting the magician archetype is "The Adventures of Merlin," a BBC miniseries. This isn't the same show we've been referencing until now, albeit the Merlin character is based on the same person. But in this case, Merlin is the understudy, not the wily, seasoned veteran we've been dissecting.

In the first episode, young Merlin arrives in Camelot. After arriving at the home of the court's physician to the king, the physician reads a letter from Merlin's mother. What she writes includes the essence of the magician's archetypal energy. She pleads to the physician to take Merlin under his wing and writes that Merlin needs "A hand to hold, a voice to guide... someone that might help him find a purpose for his gifts."

This brings us to this: *The magician archetype plays a crucial role in guiding and mentoring a young boy, walking alongside him, and encouraging him to discover the unique gifts he possesses.* This archetype is responsible for teaching the boy how to harness and utilize these talents effectively. Contrary to the notion of being born as a blank slate (tabula rasa), which some psychologists uphold, I believe we all have inherent characteristics and personality traits right from birth. The magician helps the young boy embrace and develop these inherent qualities, assisting him in his journey of self-discovery and growth.

Carl Jung expands on the idea that we all have inherent characteristics and personality traits right from birth...

Jung argues that every person is born with a unique and specific personality. As a child grows, this personality gradually reveals itself and becomes apparent. Within each individual's personality lie special gifts and talents, which are meant to be shared with the world and benefit others. These gifts are personal and differ from one individual to another.

However, with the support and guidance of the magician archetype, a powerful guiding force, these gifts can be nurtured and developed to their full potential. By embracing and honing these talents, people can discover their purpose and destiny in life, making a meaningful contribution to the world around them. The magician archetype is crucial in helping individuals unlock their inner potential, find their path, and fulfill their unique calling.

With these necessary illustrations and detours covered, let's return to my story.

As I have described, my uncle was the magician for me. My gifts included being a compassionate listener and guiding people as they seek their deeper Self. I think my mother could see that early on in me. She saw and took advantage to cathect unto me at too young of an age. I was a child then and was not ready for this type of listening.

My uncle, though, guided me with his example. I could hear how he spoke to his parishioners and the compassion that oozed out of him as he employed his gifts in the world.

And it seemed that all this rubbed off on him from his father.

His father – my grandfather before him – was also a healer. My grandfather was a psychiatric nurse in Cuba, and he continued his nursing career after he immigrated to the United States three years before the Castro Revolution. Healing then, I imagine, is a part of my family line. It is in our blood, you could say.

Spending those summers with my uncle, I had the chance to fully watch and capture how he listened and communicated as he healed. Those memories are embedded in my mind and the behavior I observe I repeat in my head when I am in session with my clients. I learned those deeper lessons while dusting, vacuuming, running around the woods, and riding down the river in an inner tube during those summers years ago.

As an adult, the healing experiences for me have been, in my work as a psychologist and becoming an analyst, being with the client in their world as they suffer. Being with them, I can see the forces that arise from the unconscious and help them experience it for themselves.

This is done very carefully, for if they are not ready, it could do more harm than good. It is very similar to when a certain type of medication is given to destroy a pathogen, and the body is not ready; the medication can kill both the host and pathogen alike.

The magician archetype's energy can *bring healing by creating a safe and supportive environment*, a 'container,' so to speak. The human unconscious mind is a reservoir of powerful and unprocessed energy. Releasing this energy without proper guidance or containment can lead to harmful and destructive outcomes.

The magician serves as a *container* or *channel* for this raw energy, guiding its flow in a constructive direction. By offering a safe space for exploration and expression, the magician allows others to navigate and process their unconscious energies healthily and productively, leading to healing and personal growth. This containment of raw energy within the influence of the magician archetype helps individuals transform and harness their inner potential for positive outcomes.

Let's now examine the magician's role as an "insulator."

The Magician as the "Insulator"

A CLIENT I SAW REPORTED that when he loses control over his anger, it is as if another person took over. He was afraid he might have a double personality coming through and that he was possessed or even going crazy. The unconscious holds intense and unprocessed energies that, when unleashed, can easily dominate behavior and override rational thought. Afterward, the person may feel drained and emotionally overwhelmed as they deal with the consequences of their actions. It's important to recognize that such experiences do not necessarily indicate a split personality or insanity but rather highlight the potency of untamed emotions and the need to explore and manage these unconscious energies constructively.

This brings us to the following: The magician's energy can act like a transformer or insulation for this type of energy.

Let me elaborate some more on this.

I have done my electrical work at home, installing ceiling fans and changing light switches. I am always aware of some basic safety precautions: wear rubber-soled shoes and ensure the circuit has been closed or turned off to the object you are working with. I remember to tap the wire to see if there is a spark, etc. The definition, then, of an insulator is a material that does not respond to an electric field and completely resists the flow of an electric charge. With this definition in mind, *the magician does not respond or react to the energy coming forth.*

With this lesson in mind, it is especially vital that psychologists and therapists embody this archetype.

One of the things psychologists and therapists, in general, learn is to be objective and not respond to the behaviors of the client/patient. This, of course, becomes increasingly difficult, especially if the therapist is not aware or disregards that there is an unconscious. If the unconscious is disregarded, the therapist is not in tune with the magician's energy and is, therefore, at risk of being sucked into the raw energy and no longer serving as an insulator.

When you are an insulator, you can be exposed to the energy but simultaneously maintain resistance to the flow of energy, or, in other words, resist identifying with or being carried away by the energy, as when a client has a reaction and the analyst remains calm and simply observes.

We all can be insulators, and what a peaceful world it would be if we were. Let's get back to my example...

When clients tell me what they have regretted doing and, most importantly, wish not to do again, I tell them about the image of the raging river. When a river is raging, and the currents are strong, it is futile and downright stupid to think we can be in the water going against the current. We will be taken away much to our own peril. What is important is to get out of the water as quickly as possible and onto the banks. From there, we can see the river from above and watch the currents flow by. From there, we can decide how to deal with the river and our next course of action.

This is a way of being an insulator for ourselves by not responding to the raw energy that comes forth, in other words, developing and being an "observing ego."

St. Ignatius of Loyola had some astute teachings on the same.

St. Ignatius of Loyola shared valuable teachings about maintaining a neutral stance when confronted with challenges or important choices. He emphasized the concept of "discerning the spirits," which means recognizing and understanding the emotions or influences that guide us toward good or evil intentions.

The key is to refrain from hasty judgments and decisions, allowing oneself to stay impartial and open-minded. By adopting this neutral position, you can avoid being swayed by impulsive emotions or biases. Instead, you patiently wait for clarity to emerge, seeking a deeper understanding of the situation or inner guidance before taking action. This approach promotes thoughtful and wise decision-making, enabling you to align your choices with what is genuinely good and beneficial for yourself and others.

Carl Jung refers to this as not choosing between two opposites. Jung suggests holding the tension, being the insulator, and waiting until a third thing arises in the form of a symbol or creative solution. Jung refers to this as the transcendent function that leads us to another level and, therefore, resolves the conflict.

The insulator slows down the energetic bandwidth to a point where it can be stated that it resists the energetic flow. When we consciously hold back and control the energy or tension within a situation, we can effectively put things into slow motion. This slowdown allows us to step back, observe, and reflect on what is happening more clearly. It allows us to better understand the situation and make informed decisions based on careful observation.

Lately, it is pretty interesting to see a visual effect used frequently in movies, where an action is shown, and then it slows down so the audience can see what is happening. This builds up the momentum or excitement in the action; in another sense, it serves as a form of insulation.

I do this for clients in sessions. When a story is told, it seems to go very fast. I break down the story and slow it down by asking questions to explore the intricacies in more detail. By doing this, it allows the individual to reflect on the occurrence, and this allows insight to surface.

The "Ah ha" moment inevitably occurs, and another dimension opens up, allowing for change and growth. This is how life is processed. That is why so many of us, when faced with a significant experience such as the death of a loved one, must tell and retell the story many times over and over.

This allows the event to slow down, and healing can occur by slowly processing what occurred. Slowing the event down, it becomes digestible, and the psyche can absorb it.

I feel that with the example I just gave above about losing a loved one, it is important that I touch on trauma and digesting/insulating against it a little bit as we wrap up this particular sub-chapter:

Trauma is an event that happens so quickly and intensely that our mind cannot process it all at once. It's like gulping down large pieces of food without chewing, leading to an upset stomach. Similarly, when we experience trauma, the overwhelming emotions and information are swallowed up without being properly understood or integrated. It is crucial to "chew" on the experience, to take time to process it, and allow ourselves to feel the emotions and thoughts associated with it. Just as we savor a meal before swallowing, slowing down the process of dealing with a traumatic event helps us digest and make sense of it, insulating us against it and leading to a healthier recovery and emotional well-being.

Now, look at the magician's role as the "transformer."

The Magician as the Transformer

THE MAGICIAN'S ENERGY also has to do with being a transformer.

The definition of a transformer is a device that transfers electrical energy from one circuit to another, and in doing so, the energy is changed.

In ancient times, mortals knew they could not confront God face to face. They knew that God was like raw energy and would instantly consume them if God just appeared with all God's glory.

We see this in the Greek myth of Hera and Semele.

In the Greek myth of Hera and Semele, the story unfolds with Hera, the powerful and jealous wife of Zeus, discovering that Semele, a mortal queen, is pregnant with Zeus's child. Fueled by jealousy and anger, Hera devises a cunning plan to avenge Semele. She disguises herself as an elderly nurse and befriends Semele, gaining her trust over time. Once she gains Semele's confidence, Hera plants the idea in Semele's mind to request Zeus to reveal his true divine form or glory as proof of his love.

Naively, Semele agrees to Hera's advice and approaches Zeus with her request. Reluctantly, Zeus gives in to her plea, unaware of Hera's manipulation in the background. When Zeus reveals his glory to Semele, his divine thunderbolts and overwhelming presence prove too much for her mortal form to bear. The intense divine energy disintegrates her, and Semele tragically meets her demise.

What was lacking here was not only insulation but also a transformer. When Zeus was covered up in his disguise, the raw god energy could be transformed to make it life-giving, hence Semele's pregnancy.

But without the proper transformer, she was instantly destroyed.

The magician archetype provides this type of lesson as well as training.

In the father's role, the magician's energy represents a powerful force that enables fathers to lead by example and teach their children how to navigate the world effectively. A significant aspect of this guidance is the teaching of creating a *persona* like a mask or transformer. This persona is a valuable tool that allows us to adapt and present ourselves in socially acceptable or professional ways to the world. It helps us interact with others and live harmoniously in a civilized society.

Without this essential function, we would be emotionally raw and exposed, potentially harming our relationships rather than strengthening them. The father's role in teaching the persona is crucial in shaping the child's ability to connect with others and function well in the world.

The magician's energy empowers fathers to teach their children through their actions, showing them how to construct a persona. This persona acts as a transformative mask that enables us to fit into society and maintain positive relationships. Without it, we would struggle to connect with others and navigate the complexities of social life. Thus, the father's instilling this understanding is pivotal in helping children become well-adjusted and capable individuals worldwide.

As a psychologist and professional, I wear my persona while presenting a composed and professional version of myself. This is essential because if I were to express my inner thoughts, emotions, and desires in their raw form, it could be harmful to the relationship I have with my clients. Having my persona in place, I can create a safe and supportive environment for my clients to share their feelings and thoughts without feeling overwhelmed or judged. It allows me to maintain appropriate boundaries and provide effective guidance without letting my issues interfere with the therapy process. Ultimately, wearing a persona ensures I can be a helpful and reliable psychologist, promoting trust and positive outcomes for my clients.

Let's expound on the transformer concept some more.

In today's world, authenticity is often cherished and encouraged, but it's crucial to recognize that a balance is required between inner thoughts and outward expression. We need a transformer that acts like a filter or mask to manage the difference between our inner "voltage" (thoughts, emotions, desires) and the external voltage in the world. This transformer helps us adjust our interactions with others, allowing us to navigate social situations with sensitivity and understanding. Expressing every raw thought could lead to misunderstandings, conflicts, and damaged relationships without this filter. While it's essential to be true to ourselves, employing the appropriate transformer ensures we can relate to others effectively and maintain harmonious connections.

For instance, consider the scenario of speaking your mind without any filter. If we say everything we are thinking without considering the impact on others, it could lead to detrimental consequences. Our relationships might suffer, especially with our loving partners, friends, and even family. People might find our unfiltered honesty hurtful or offensive, and this could result in strained or broken connections. While honesty is essential, using the right transformer allows us to express ourselves thoughtfully, choose words wisely, and maintain healthy relationships with the people we care most about.

The transformer, thus, is there for us to translate a thought into words that could still carry the message but perhaps in a softer, gentler tone.

We very briefly touched on the magician archetype and the container role. However, it was necessary to explore the other roles first, as they led to this one. Let's now explore the magician's role as the "container."

The Magician as the Container

THE MAGICIAN'S ENERGY involves the concept of the container, which refers to anything capable of holding the powerful and raw energy of our inner forces or unconscious mind. Think of the container as a vessel that can safely hold and channel these intense emotions, desires, and thoughts within us.

This container could be a person's coping mechanisms, artistic expressions, rituals, or any structured activity allowing us to constructively process and harness our inner energies. Understanding and utilizing the container can prevent these powerful forces from becoming overwhelming or destructive. Instead, we can find ways to channel them in a balanced and productive manner. The container is crucial in helping us manage and integrate our unconscious aspects, leading to personal growth and a deeper understanding of ourselves.

The container is not only a vessel for holding raw energy but is also akin to a sacred space, a temenos that houses the numinous or divine essence within us. It represents a state of being where we have control over our impulses. When we are contained, we can manage our actions, thoughts, and emotions in a balanced way. However, in today's world, we often lack access to the magician archetype and its empowering energy, which leads to a rise in impulsiveness and hyperactivity. Without the container and the guidance of the magician's energy, we may struggle to control our impulses and find it challenging to maintain a sense of inner balance, resulting in impulsive behaviors and a lack of focus. Embracing the container and tapping into the magician's energy is crucial for fostering self-control and maintaining a more centered and grounded approach to life.

In recent studies dealing with emotional intelligence, the ability to delay gratification is a trait of higher intelligence. These studies indicate that if one can hold one's impulses and not act or concretize them, then this strengthens the individual's intellect.

Therefore, impulse control is part and parcel of the magician's realm.

Let me give a personal story to help elaborate on what we've just covered:

In many traditions, there are liturgical seasons where one is expected to fast. During these seasons, it is customary to give up something. For example, I use the season of Lent to give up certain foods and participate in a cleansing diet.

Since childhood, I have suffered from allergies, and taking an antihistamine was part of my daily diet. I was referred to a Chinese doctor who, at my first consultation, prescribed that I cleanse for 35 days before she gave me herbs for my allergies. I followed her prescribed diet, and in doing so, I learned about having discipline over my body, especially my cravings for starches and sugar substitutes.

I had to give up drinking espresso, bread containing gluten and yeast, sugar substitutes, sugar in all forms, milk, cheese, red meat, and many other things I loved eating. The result was that I could master my cravings and free myself from taking antihistamines. I lost weight, and most importantly, my creativity flourished as I had to learn new ways of cooking and eating.

These ritual seasons, as well as sacred spaces that, more often than not, call for impulse control, are part of the realm of the magician archetype.

Let's now look at the magician and the "observing ego."

The Magician and the 'Observing Ego'"

THE MAGICIAN'S ENERGY deals with exploring the unknown, the mysterious, and the uncommon.

In other words, the magician's energy deals with insight and being aware or conscious of something.

What we in the mental health field call the "observing ego," or as I like to call it, the ego that observes rather than is caught up, is also part of the magician's archetypal energy.

The ego, the part of us we know as us and are aware of to some degree, is very important for our daily living. The function of a healthy ego is one of being aware or observing our environments. I use the word environments in the plural because I like to include the inner world of thoughts, emotions, physical symptoms, and the outer environment around us. The ego's job, then, is to be conscious of, experiencing, and observing these environments as best as possible.

When the ego's observing stance is interrupted, it is a good indicator that something has grabbed hold of it, or as I mentioned earlier, the ego is caught up. In-depth psychology is described as a complex or archetypal possession.

An archetype is a basic pattern or characteristic that many people share. It's a way of being or behaving that's common among humans. On the other hand, a complex is a mix of thoughts, memories, and feelings connected to a core idea linked to the archetype. In neuroscience, this connection is similar to how neurons in the brain form networks. These fragmented memories are experiences that hold emotions and can be triggered by things like pictures, smells, or short movie-like scenes of events. So, an archetype is like a fundamental energy of common human traits, while a complex is a collection of personal memories and emotions tied to that archetype, and it's all linked together like networks are in the brain.

Let's examine a movie example to illustrate the points better.

In the movie, "What the Bleep Do I Know?", there is a segment where memories are described as holographic images in the brain. These images are found in the neuronal nets found in the brain. Millions of these neurons in the brain form nets, which are simply neurons joining together in a cluster. These neurons contain memories of events in our past. When you recall any memory, usually, there is an accompanying emotion.

This is what a complex is like in psychological terms. The more you explore memory, the more you will find that the memory is linked to other similar types of memories, all having similar emotions that arise. The linkage of memories appears to have a common theme or element. This common theme points to a common energy, which is the archetype.

I think of a balloon filled with memories that stir up emotions inside, and the center or core of the balloon is a central theme or archetype. This central theme is common to all humanity, no matter the culture. It is universal. For example, some common themes are mother, father, brothers and sisters, birth, death, relationships, sex, etc. Understanding this was helpful in my developing an ego that observes.

As you can imagine, these events and memories are felt powerfully. When they are touched upon, we have an emotional reaction. We are choked up, cannot speak, forget what we were thinking or saying, or get teary-eyed. This is what it is like when a complex takes hold of the ego. In that moment, we lose our awareness of our environment and could even live that memory as if we were there.

There are degrees of strength in the ego being caught up by the complex. Sometimes, it is weak, and we can regain control again, and at other times, we cannot help but allow the tears to flow, and we can no longer speak a word. Another example is when dealing with impulsivity or inability to contain rage.

The magician's energy is available to deal with this. It helps in assisting a developing observing ego. The ego needs to get out of the way of a complex or archetype when the energy is strong enough to come forth into consciousness. As I stated earlier with the river metaphor, when a complex or archetype comes forth, and the river rages, we must get out, fast!

Years ago, I visited Puerto Rico's Yunque National Park. There is a river there where people like to go and bathe. One of the locals there informed me that they know that when the water level suddenly lowers, it is an indicator to get out of the river—pronto! If not, a raging current comes down the mountain like a tsunami, and you could be washed away to your death.

Similar dynamics apply concerning the observing ego.

The observing ego is a way of getting out of the river and onto the banks. From there, you can watch the raging river flow, acknowledge it, and observe it from a safe enough distance. If not, you will be identified with the complex energy, think the anger, sadness, or whatever other emotion you are having is really you, and get caught up wherever the complex takes you.

Remember the client I brought up, who explained that it is as if another person takes over when he gets enraged? When some people get very angry, they find it difficult to stay in control, and it feels like someone else is in charge of their actions. This is a common problem for those with trouble managing their anger.

To address this issue, certain anger management groups attempt to help individuals by strengthening their egos and teaching them various techniques to manage and restrain their anger. In Puerto Rico, people use the phrase "Me sale el monstro," which translates to "the monster comes out," to describe this experience. This comparison to a monster is powerful because the intense anger can seem like a frightening and uncontrollable beast taking over a person's behavior, similar to how a wild and ferocious monster would act.

I enjoyed watching the T.V. show The Incredible Hulk as a child, for example. When Dr. Banner becomes angry, the complex, represented by the Hulk, completely dominates, and Dr. Banner's true self seems to disappear. This occurrence demonstrates how the ego is overwhelmed by the powerful and uncontrollable force of the complex.

For individuals who struggle with anger and rage, they understand the consequences of allowing their "Incredible Hulk" to emerge. Just like the destructive nature of the Hulk, giving in to these intense emotions can lead to significant damage and adverse outcomes. Therefore, addressing and managing these complexes effectively becomes crucial to avoid harmful consequences and maintain control over one's actions and emotions.

The Ego, the Self & the Magician's Role in Both

WE'VE SPOKEN AT LENGTH about the observing ego.

The ego plays a crucial role in our minds. It acts like a lookout, scanning the world and our inner thoughts and feelings. It's like a wise observer, keeping track of everything happening inside and outside us. After gathering all this information, it uses its intelligence to guide our energy in the right direction. The ego's goal is to help us make well-informed decisions, where we are fully aware of what's going on and what's best for us.

Imagine the ego as a filter, sifting through all the incoming data and sorting out the relevant and vital bits. It helps us see the bigger picture, giving us a better understanding of our situations. By doing so, the ego allows us to make choices based on reason and consciousness rather than acting on impulse or emotion. This way, we can make better decisions that align with our values and goals, leading to a more balanced and fulfilling life.

The ego does this by aligning with what Carl Jung termed the *Self*.

In Jung's view, the Self is like the big boss of our minds. It's not just a center; it includes everything within us, both the things we're aware of (consciousness) and those we aren't (unconsciousness). The Self brings order and unity to our entire inner world. It's like the heart that holds everything together. On the other hand, the ego is more like a center within our conscious mind. It's the "I" or "me" we identify with, but it's not the same as the Self. The Self stands on its own, like the idea of a higher power or our higher self.

Jung believed that the Self is like a connecting force that links us to the concept of a divine presence. It's this sense of something bigger than us, spiritual or god-like that we can experience through the Self. So, while the ego is a part of our conscious identity, the Self is this larger, all-encompassing aspect that goes beyond our individuality and connects us to something higher or more profound.

Imagine the ego, which is like our sense of self or "I," and the Self, which is this bigger, all-encompassing aspect, like two separate centers within us. When they connect and interact, it forms what Jungians call the "ego-Self Axis." This connection is like any relationship with someone else; it's essential for our psychological well-being. Both the ego and the Self are independent and have roles, so how they relate to each other matters.

The relationship between the ego and the Self is often complicated, and it's reflected in religious myths where humans seek a connection with a Creator, a higher power, or the God-image. Our psychological growth and development are heavily influenced by how this ego-to-Self relationship evolves and changes. It's a significant part of our journey towards self-discovery and understanding our place in the grand scheme of things. As this relationship develops, we can experience personal growth and a deeper sense of purpose and meaning in life. I'm hoping I've done an adequate job of explaining this as best as possible without being overly technical or using "psychobabble."

During the first half of life, the ego must develop by separating from the Self. However, the second half of life requires a surrender or relativization of the ego as it experiences and relates to the Self.

The role of the magician's archetypal energy is to guide the ego to the Self and initiate it into the world of secret wisdom, which it will need to make informed decisions. The ego is described as being a servant to the Self, carrying out behaviors in the real world or in the individual's life. I perceive this to be the case in boys being initiated into men.

This is the magician archetype, like a priest who teaches us the mysteries of God or a wise grandfather who can tell us the secrets of living.

Let's listen back to my personal story.

Until that first summer with my uncle, I only knew of two fathers: my stepfather, the tyrant, and my real father, whom we will discuss in the next chapter. I needed magician archetypal energy to begin guiding me into the mysteries of the Self or God.

Ironically, my uncle, a minister, had much of this energy. My uncle first told me that I would have to one day move away from home if I wanted to grow up and be a man. That concept was initially very disturbing to me. I had always been very close to my mother, and how could I leave her behind? I recall hearing him and thinking I would never let this happen. I thought as a child that I would live with my mother forever.

Years later, while living in Australia for one year, I remembered my uncle's words. There I was on the other side of the world, as far as I could get from my mother for a year! Even Christmas was spent Down Under! How right my uncle was, for it is there in the land beyond the black stump that I began an initiation into manhood.

Another magician took over my uncle's role there, Dan, my boss, and minister, whom I introduced you to in the first chapter. Remember that wonderful gentleman who helped me come to grips with my homosexuality? Well, I left out a few things about him in Chapter 1, as they were irrelevant to the points I was trying to bring across...

Dan was a man who had suffered physically. He had had a brain tumor and had undergone surgery, leaving him unable to walk without crutches. Despite this, he had a wonderful spirit. In Australia, I began coming out and facing my sexual orientation. As you know, I confessed to Dan that I was gay and described my struggle. He could take the bolt of energy I released on him and transform it into something positive, facilitating my growth.

Allow me to repeat some things Dan asked me, which I covered in Chapter 1. They need repeating as I need to illustrate an important point:

His first instruction and advice was that if I continued to be an assistant and youth pastor in his parish, I must not engage in any sexual acts or visit any places that would increase the risk of a scandal. He asked me if I could promise him that. I understood that he did this not to protect his name and authority or even to protect the church; rather, he said this to insulate me from the negative energy that would follow if, indeed, a scandal occurred. I understood this, and I was immensely grateful. I kept my promise and remained faithful to my work at the time, maintaining my celibacy.

It required a good amount of Pastor Dan's magician archetypal energy to hold this tension for me and guide me through this difficult time. I was too "small," just beginning to bud in my journey to being more of myself.

This reminds me of the parable of the seeds in the New Testament. Some seeds were thrown on the rocks, and the worries of this world choked them and prevented them from sprouting and growing. The birds took other seeds.

Dan was protecting my seeds.

Young and newborn, if any scandal broke out, the damage that would have taken place would have been horrendous, and the journey to ultimately accepting and being proud of my gay self would have been so much more convoluted. I may never have gotten to where I am.

The aid of this other magician guided me, and now, looking back, I am so thankful.

The Magician, & Canalization and Calcination

THE MAGICIAN'S ENERGY is also available to ensure proper channeling or "canalization," as Jung calls it. Canalization is taken from the idea of water canals channeled through a landscape.

I grew up in Miami, and we have many canals. If not for the canals, then the land would be swampy and unstable. The canals keep the water in its place and guide the water, distributing it appropriately.

Jung used this term in much the same way. The energy has to be channeled so that it is directed in a manner that is the most useful to the psyche or psychological functioning, we can also say.

The role of the magician archetype is also to help instruct how this can be done and be in the world. If proper canalization is not performed, one will act out their impulses and desires without regard to the consequences.

I frequently witness both children and adults acting out. It is as if the idea of authenticity is stated as an excuse for acting out. Holding back in some way is viewed as repression and, therefore, unhealthy or even primitive.

Repression is like a protective shield that our mind puts up without realizing. It happens automatically, without conscious thought. It's a way for our minds to hide or push away thoughts, feelings, or memories that might be distressing. Because of this, repression is inherently negative. On the other hand, when we choose not to act on something, it's a conscious decision that comes from careful thinking. It's not a hidden or automatic process like repression; rather, it's a deliberate and healthy way to handle our emotions and complex feelings.

Deciding not to act out allows us to channel our emotions constructively. Instead of reacting impulsively, we take the time to reflect on the situation and consciously choose not to act on our initial impulses. This helps us avoid unnecessary conflicts or harm to ourselves and others. It's a mature way of dealing with our emotions and energy, promoting emotional intelligence and better relationships with others.

With this covered, I'd like to lean on alchemy for a bit and explore the subject of calcination.

In alchemy, alchemists use calcination to transform base metals into something more valuable by adding heat flames to the material for it to dry. The psychological idea of calcination is similar. The idea is that by refraining from acting out, it can also feel like one is under fire.

One can feel as if one is burning because the desire to act on an impulse is so strong. But this symbolic act of burning melts away the excess and volatile elements of the personality, leaving a stronger, drier, essential core.

Whenever we have gone through a period of trials, we have said that we were baptized by fire, or in plain English, it was hell! This describes the fires of "calcination." The magician archetype guides the child through this process. As a result, the child can live in the world more consciously and wholly integrated. This process of holding back our desires transforms us into individuals who can better hold tension, develop more self-control, and relate better to others, especially the other that is our Self.

We feel intact and more connected with our true essence when we do not just act out indiscriminately.

This brings us to an important question: How do we combine these last two concepts of canalization and calcination?

I would like to suggest that we can first learn to contain and hold the desire or tension we are experiencing. I use the word experiencing because some of us feel it, and others are caught up in thoughts, as in obsessive thinking. That is a good beginning if we can hold the tension and strong, intense desire and maintain control of our actions and decisions.

Once this is done and the emotions are held, we can begin the process of canalizing. One way this can be accomplished is by separating or differentiating what is being experienced. By differentiating, we are beginning to draw or channel out some of the energy. There's a technique that therapists use to the same end:

One technique they use is to try to get the client to describe what they are experiencing using images or metaphors. This process adds structure, draws out the energy, and projects it onto a metaphor or image. Describing it as something outside of ourselves is a first step to begin to relate to it consciously. This process using alchemical terms is called *separatio* because we are separating the experience from who we "are" and increasingly gaining some objective perspective.

By first holding the tension and desire and then drawing from it through separating and differentiating the experience into various elements, our consciousness is increased, and we make better decisions, resulting in more effective actions.

This is a way of fully manifesting our true essence in the world, which is what the magician archetype is meant to teach us.

Wrapping Up

WITH MEN LIKE MY UNCLE and Dan, I have come to appreciate the magician archetype being present in my life. I also realize how the magician archetype is active in the work with my clients.

In today's world, we need magician archetypal energy, and we need men to allow this energy to flow through them. Children need guidance on how to be in the world, not only to be prepared for facing life's challenges but also to better express themselves and make a more solid impact.

We all bring our unique energy meant to transform and recreate the world. Humanity needs our uniqueness to fulfill its destiny.

When we allow the magician archetype to be present through us, we are doing our part in the evolution of humankind.

This chapter is, quite unsurprisingly, the longest of them all, as it is this particular archetype that shaped the man I have become today. I am ever so grateful to the magicians in my life – my uncle and Pastor Dan – and hope that I can do for others what these men did for me.

Next up, I explore my biological father and the masculine archetype he embodied.

Let's reflect before we move on to the next archetype:

Who was the magician for you in your life? What lessons did you learn from them?

How have you experienced "insulation, transformer, and container" in your experience? Did you relate to my experience of holding onto burning desire and wanting to throw in the towel and take action?

What are your thoughts about being authentic and impulsive, throwing off the mask of persona, or getting rid of your filter? What do you see in others' behaviors?

What thoughts, impressions, and emotions arose as you read this chapter? Even if you disagree, I invite you to look at that.

Chapter 5: The Lover Archetype-
My Father

Photo by Jack Hamilton

And finally, I get to my father's archetype – the lover. I have been resisting writing concerning my father, and maybe consciously or unconsciously, that is why I have left him for later in the book.

When I think about my dad, I go immediately to a time when we played catch under a mango tree in his backyard. He was a former player for the

Baltimore Orioles, and he always dreamed I would also have the same passion for baseball, but I never did.

In my memories of him, the first image that comes to my mind is of him throwing me the ball, and I try my best to catch it (and often fail to).

My father embodied the archetype of the lover through and through.

Growing up, I never once heard my father reprimanding me for how I spoke, where I put my hands, or how straight my wrist was. Only once did he question me. He asked if playing the piano would make my hands soft.

His question was one of concern, yet indirect to be gentle with me.

It was my mother and stepfather, on the other hand, who constantly corrected and reprimanded me for my mannerisms.

In my eyes, my father was gentle, kind, and very affectionate. For him, it was not wrong to hug me and kiss me, even in public. I could feel the warmth of his hands and even recall his lips as he put my fingers into his mouth.

Mind you, nothing sexual here. Sensual, yes, as my father was all about the five senses in how he showed his affection. He embodied the lover archetype as wholly as anyone can.

Dissecting the Lover Archetype

THE LOVER ARCHETYPE symbolizes the energies linked to the male reproductive organ, the phallus. In ancient Greece, wealthy families had a peculiar feature in their gardens: a large phallus-like structure representing the god Priapus. While this might seem unusual to us today, it held significance as a representation of the life force and divine energy carried by the blood in many ancient civilizations. In Jungian terms, when this life force, also known as libido, flows into the fleshy appendix and boosts it upwards, it signifies the ultimate fusion of spirit into flesh. The erect penis was seen as a clear indication that this life force was present and active.

So, the lover archetype goes beyond mere physical attraction and sexuality. It symbolizes the vital force that animates life and connects the spiritual with the material. In ancient times, the representation of the phallus in the garden was considered a potent symbol of this life force, but it might be perceived quite differently in today's context. Nonetheless, the underlying concept of the lover archetype remains about the union of spirit and flesh, representing the life-affirming energies that underpin creation and the perpetuation of life itself.

When I first reflected on this, I was taken back to a verse in the book of John, in the New Testament, "The Word was made flesh," referring to Christ. The Word or *logos*, which can denote spirit, came into the flesh, the material, and became one with the material or flesh.

This is precisely the mystery or the numinosity the Greeks associated with the erect penis, so much so that it became a sign for their god.

In one of its temples, the Hindu religion also has a phallus formed out of rock as a sign of the god Shiva, the creator and destroyer of the earth. The ancient civilizations knew that behind the erect penis was a mystery not being spoken and thus sacred, the symbol of coagulatio.

I've leaned on alchemy multiple times up to this point. And I will yet again below.

The Lover Archetype and the "Coagulatio" Concept

IN ALCHEMY, ONE OF the operations the alchemists used when working with metal was called *coagulatio*, which is the solidification of a metal or another type of substance. In this process, shape and form were given to either a solution, liquid form, or gaseous form. A material became hardened if the liquid was evaporated or it was kept soft and malleable like mud.

In the work of analysis, the coagulatio or coagulation stage can be seen when a thought or idea is put into an observable action. When a shape is given to something abstract as a feeling or thought, coagulatio is also used.

A little detour...

Carl Jung found alchemy's processes incredibly useful as metaphors in his analytical work. When discussing our emotions or thoughts, merely staying at a vague, abstract level isn't helpful. Instead, he utilized alchemical symbols and concepts to delve deeper into the unconscious mind, understanding the transformative processes and hidden meanings behind human experiences. By embracing these metaphors, Jung believed individuals could gain profound insights and better comprehend their inner selves.

Now, let me give a story about a client I had so we can better understand the coagulation concept...

I had a client who would become paralyzed when she was under stress.

In one session, I asked her to describe the stress. At first, she looked puzzled, and then, after a few seconds of silence, she began to describe a dark tornado coming down from the sky. It began to tear up the land, making its way towards her. It was helpful for her to begin dealing with the imaginary tornado as we would if a real tornado came down from the sky and headed our way.

We did some active imagination, a technique used in the analytical method, and slowly, her paralysis subsided. She allowed herself to run and seek shelter.

Using a metaphor or coagulation is much like the blood moving through the arteries, veins, and capillaries that erect the penis. The blood gives life to the penis, as it were, and the metaphor brings to life what is formless in the emotion or the symptom.

In this way, the lover archetype carries the operation of coagulation and metaphor.

One could say that in biology or physiology, a baby is also an example of "coagulation." It starts with a desire between two people. They unite in sexual intercourse, and the desire for each other materializes in a fertilized egg, which becomes an embryo soon after a fetus. The desire or thought took shape and became a life of its own.

The lover archetype embodies this unification, this energy and spirit, desire into matter, and then we have a physical life coming into being.

The Lover – A Difficult Archetype

THE LOVER ARCHETYPE is a difficult archetypal energy to deal with.

It is uncomfortable in a way, and to the same degree of discomfort, some will feel when they read the description of my father putting my fingers into his mouth and how I recall his full lips covering my fingers, leaving them moist.

Even in history, we can see how the lover archetype has been challenged, persecuted, and attempts made to eliminate it from conscious human life.

In Christian Europe during the Middle Ages, people linked to the lover archetype, like artists, musicians, actors, playwrights, and alchemists, were often pushed to the edges of society. They faced marginalization and were labeled as followers of the Devil or being driven by evil desires. Those who expressed strong emotions or had a deep connection with nature were accused of witchcraft or sorcery. The discomfort these individuals' closeness to their world caused in others led to attempts to punish and banish them from mainstream society.

These individuals were seen as different and threatening because they represented a departure from the strict norms of the time. Some misunderstood and feared their creativity and emotional depth, leading to unjust persecution and discrimination. It was a time when conformity was highly valued, and anyone who deviated from the expected norms faced harsh consequences. However, as time progressed, society began to recognize the value of these individuals' contributions, and many of the artistic, creative, and emotional expressions that were once condemned are now celebrated as essential aspects of human culture and expression. Nevertheless, even in modern society, they still face considerable problems and challenges.

Throughout my life, I have had a deep fascination with stories about saints and mystics. Among them, the tale of Teresa of Avila has captivated me the most. Her life and spiritual journey have been a source of inspiration, and I have found myself drawn to the profound wisdom and experiences she shared. Teresa's story highlights her extraordinary connection with the divine, unwavering faith, and dedication to a higher purpose. Learning about her struggles, visions, and profound insights has enriched my spiritual understanding and motivated me to explore my relationship with the sacred and mystical in life.

On a trip to Rome a couple of years ago with my partner, I recall walking into the church of Santa Maria Vitoria, and immediately, my eyes were drawn to the marble statue of Saint Teresa of Avila and the angel.

The saint's expression drew me to reflect on sexual desire and recall moments of orgasm. At first, I felt slightly ashamed, but I continued to think and reflect. Yes, for me, sex has always been something that has taken me closer to the Divine.

Here's a confession that you may either find hilarious or quite unsettling. Or both...

There have been times when I was having sex with my partner that I would, without conscious effort on my part, sing praises. This made my partner uneasy. He wondered, what was I saying? Worse yet, he thought we might both be struck by lightning in the middle of the bed.

What a horrible way to die. Or was it?

Back to Saint Teresa of Avila, the image of this holy woman before me at that church in Rome was such a wonderful image of the lover archetype and the uniting of spirit and matter, of being one with something bigger and allowing oneself to enjoy the felt union.

Away from saints and such kind, I'd like to give a story of my father and me and use it to examine a couple of traits of the lover's masculine archetype. But rather than tell the story first, I'll lay out these traits and then get to the story for illustration.

The Lover Archetype: Vitality, Passion, and Tapping into All Five Senses

THE LOVER'S ARCHETYPAL energy encompasses qualities that make a person feel vibrant, passionate, and full of life. When you embody these traits, it becomes evident to others around you.

On the contrary, the absence of the lover archetype can leave you feeling dull, lifeless, and devoid of creativity and spontaneity. It's like the difference between radiating vitality and being void of it. This archetype influences our emotions, relationships, and our ability to engage with the world around us. Understanding and embracing the lover's archetypal energy can lead to a more fulfilling and expressive life while neglecting it can lead to stagnation, barrenness, and emotional disconnect.

Storytime...

Recalling my father, I can remember vividly times when he was alive, full of passion and life. My father lit up when talking about baseball, his international currency collection, or the grains of wood in lumber.

When I was about ten, my father asked if I wanted to work at his lumber company. I thought it would be exciting when I said yes. My father's company was this large warehouse filled with towers of lumber. One-third of the warehouse was separated for carpentry work, where kitchen cabinets and moldings were made. I was fascinated by watching the machine intricately design the grooves and round sides, resulting in what I thought was a work of art.

My father took me around the warehouse on various occasions to educate me on the various types of wood he had. He would take a slab of lumber and show me the grain design and color. He explained that with each grain and color, one could tell what type of wood it was.

To this day, I can tell more or less what type of wood I am looking at by the grain. I can close my eyes and recall touching the wood, always going with the grain to avoid getting splinters and breathing in the smell of wood.

Since my favorite color is red, I loved any wood that had the word red in its name or had a rose tint. Red oak, cherry, and mahogany were my favorite woods.

My father had a way of really being connected with his five senses, especially touch. I learned more in those young days about the smell of wood when cut or how pine felt softer on my skin than the other types of wood.

What would have happened if my stepfather had taken the same approach and educated me on silkscreening? Two different men with two different masculine archetypal energies.

I worked hard at my father's company.

The lover archetype is closely tied to our five senses and how we experience life through them. In Analytical Psychology, it's known as the Sensation Function. If you've taken the Myers Briggs Type Indicator Test (MBTI), those who strongly prefer the present moment, the immediate surroundings, and the tangible experiences around them most likely, have sensation as their dominant function. They revel in the sensory richness of the here and now, valuing what they can see, touch, taste, hear, and smell. This orientation allows them to fully immerse themselves in the present experience, appreciating the beauty and details of the world vividly and engagingly.

Individuals with a dominant sensation function tend to enjoy sharing their personal stories and experiences, focusing on life's concrete and tangible aspects rather than abstract ideas. They are often described as down-to-earth and practical, having a realistic outlook on the world.

This aligns with the essence of the lover archetype, which emphasizes embracing and fully experiencing the present reality.

By immersing themselves in the here and now, these individuals can better understand reality, appreciating its beauty and significance more deeply. The lover's archetypal energy encourages them to accept and engage with what is happening now, allowing for profound personal growth and a genuine connection to the world around them.

Another example that defines the lover archetype for me is Romanticism art. Romanticism was a movement aiming to capture the natural world as it is. It was a reaction against rationalism, the industrial revolution, and disconnection. To rationalize, intellectualize, and hypothesize is to be objective and, hence, disconnected. The lover archetype is about union, acceptance, and fully experiencing life.

Back to me, living in my world of fantasies and imagination as a child was comfortable.

I grew up in the age of Star Wars, and many days, my bedspreads became landscapes of planets far, far away. What was not so easy for me was to connect with the day-to-day. Experiencing life through my senses was not my forté, let alone experiencing my body or anything that connected me to the world around me.

During adolescence, I became disconnected from my body, preferring to hide in my spirituality. I had fantasies and felt things I was told were wrong and shameful in my body. I continued to strive to be the best for God and ignore what I longed for in my body.

It was not until years later that I allowed myself to feel sexual and sensual. Years later, I began to connect with people and not only to ideas and theories. It took a while for the lover archetype to manifest in my life and for me to open the door and let him in.

It has been written, and many therapists have agreed, that heterosexual men generally fall in love with a woman who resembles their mother in many ways. It could be argued that gay men seek relationships with men who resemble their fathers in some way.

Whether there is research supporting this claim, I do not know; however, based on my experience, this might be so...

Most of my lovers and partners have been men who manifest the lover's archetypal energy. They were (and are) warm, caring, affectionate, and very much sensual men. These are the qualities I have always attributed to my father.

I consider that my father was a man of sensuality and sexuality. He carried it in the manner of how he looked, dressed, and smelled. I recall my father always smelled great after he showered. He took the time to bathe himself in his favorite cologne.

My father cared about how he looked. He was charming, extroverted, and a great conversationalist. This brings up the other trait of the lover archetype – their sensual connection and 'material' presence.

The Lover Archetype: Sensual Connection and Material Presence

THE QUALITIES OF THE lover archetype are also the energy of display, a healthy presentation of oneself, being in one's body without shame, and being fully and sensually present in the physical world.

There is a certain materialism that embodies this archetype. Materialism is not in the modern sense of hoarding or consumption, which would be a shadow quality, but in the sense of being deeply connected with the material world, what one sees, hears, and touches.

Returning to the theme of being united with the world, this energy is sensitive to the surroundings and, therefore, able to connect with them.

In my experience, I am moved by the sensual. What I see, touch, hear, etc., can transport me somewhere else, in my thoughts, ideas, memories, etc. The lover archetype, on the other hand, does not go anywhere. It stays connected with the present moment and the objects of his attention.

The objects or people that trigger his sensations are the end for him. He feels and senses all the information that comes as a result of being in tune and connected.

Here's another story for you to illustrate this better:

When my current partner Jose and I met, he was literally enthralled by my clothes, body, and good looks. This was enough for him. Yes, such things are good, but they are only important because of what they mean to me.

But Jose goes many steps further with this one – he has this way of caring for his clothes, what he sprays on his skin for odor, and how his hairstyle is shaped.

His touch revives plants, and our terrace is alive with beautiful blooms in many shapes, colors, and sizes because of him. Jose is very much connected to the lover archetype. He is practical in absolutely every sense.

In its fullness, the lover archetype is a mature masculine energy and can manifest in either gender. I'll provide yet another story to illustrate this.

I once had a dream where I was walking in a swamp. I looked down to see my feet walking literally on the water, and I could see the long grass flowing underneath. The scene was like a bayou, like the ones in Louisiana. Next to me was a woman, my contemporary in age. A fiery redhead with a motherly body, nurturing breasts, wide hips, and full legs. She wore a flowing, long, tangerine-colored dress, and she walked and danced barefoot with me on this swamp. She was very much connected to the landscape, to which she laughed in full enjoyment.

There was no thinking, intuition, or being in one's head. It was all about being in nature and enjoying walking barefoot on this watery, grassy swamp underneath large cypress trees. This was it, the fullness of the experience.

This woman in my dream, which I equate with my *anima*, also fully carried the lover's archetypal energy.

The Lover Archetypal Energy & Embodying the Being-With, Or Union Aspect

AS MENTIONED IN THE last chapter, the magician's archetypal energy includes the spiritual transforming aspect. In this chapter, the lover's archetypal energy embodies the being-with or union aspect I described earlier.

In Australia, I began to become acquainted with this energy. I was fresh out of university with a Bachelor's degree in Theology. I knew about the church's standards and doctrines, and I knew a lot about theology. These were all abstract and removed from the day-to-day human experience. Since my dominant function is intuition, studying paradigms, theories, etc., was easy. What was more challenging, though, was bringing everything I learned into the mundane and connecting with others.

In Oz, I was expected to be with young people of the local parish where I served as an assistant pastor. I remember thinking, "What good is eating dinner with folks or having long walks and discussions with young adults and adolescents?" I thought I was wasting my time and felt slightly guilty for being paid.

It was not until about six months after arriving that I relaxed and was open to the experience. I began slowly to see the value of getting to know my parishioners and having them know me.

It was connection and relationship that became important, not dogma or theology. These young people needed to see God through the church being represented via me, reaching out to them and accepting them in love.

The lover's archetypal energy was required and very much essential.

During that time, I also craved connection, as I felt lonely being in this part of the world, far away from everything familiar. It was through feeling my loneliness that allowed me to have compassion, as well as to accept other's help and companionship.

That was my first real lesson with the lover archetype.

The next lesson with this archetypal energy came in my Jungian training.

At my local seminar, a presenting analyst reviewed alchemical plates, and we arrived at one he labeled "the bath." I remember feeling the heebie-jeebies. I did not like it at all. Where were the boundaries that protected me from being contaminated in this bath?

I needed the persona of the psychologist to feel safe during the analysis, and that is where I hid. I was being asked to get into the "bath" or engage fully during the analytic hour with my clients. "No way," I thought. The process has been slow, and I feel much more accepting of the bath and being present with my clients. I feel much better about just being with them and focusing on the relationship, or what is known as the transference and alliance.

Knowing and accepting that both the analyst and the analysand are transformed in the analysis was a significant step in my growth during my training.

That is why, increasingly, I have let go of the persona of the doctor, the psychologist, and have been feeling more like the soul guide, the priest. My work resembles my time in Australia more than anything I have done under my title of doctor.

We've looked at transference in the previous masculine archetypes. And here, we will look at it again, but this time via the lens of the lover archetype.

The Lover Archetype & Transference/Counter-

Transference

IN PSYCHOLOGY, THE lover archetype is connected to concepts like transference, counter-transference, and the inter-subjective field. To truly engage with these elements, we must remain fully present and attentive to the other person, understanding their emotions and feelings deeply. This involves recognizing and addressing re-enactments of past experiences that may arise in the present, a part of the transference process.

By staying in the present moment and being attuned to these subtleties, we can be part of the transformative journey the psyche guides us towards. This approach fosters genuine connections and personal growth, allowing for a more profound understanding of ourselves and others in the therapeutic process.

I can allow intuition to enter, but if I do not remain present and engaged with the analysand, then little good can happen.

Here are a couple of examples:

It took me a long time to express that I love my clients. I used to think that attitude was unprofessional and that even saying that I loved my clients would put me at risk of acting unethically.

In one recent supervision session, I sensed my supervising analyst's intense fear that I would enact an erotic transference. I caught this and expressed it to her. She smiled and sighed, leaning back against her seat. She said that she was afraid because the erotic transference was so strong. I then smiled and said that as long as I am present and can sense that it is there, it reduces the chances I will act on it.

It requires being present, again an aspect of the lover archetype.

Another analyst once described one of his sessions with an analysand where there was an erotic transference. The analyst, to my horror at the time, spent the session exploring the attraction the analysand had towards him in detail.

Listening to the presentation felt heavy for me. I do not know how this analyst was able to do it. It felt so uncomfortable then, and now I realize that the analyst could remain engaged, in relation, and present.

In this way, the analyst could hold the tension of the erotic in the session and eventually find the meaning that fueled the passion and desire. There was a transition from the concrete to the symbolic.

As we described earlier, engaging the concrete, or the coagulatio, is a way to begin walking the path toward the symbolic.

Wrapping Up

MY FATHER SEEMED TO manifest this lover's archetypal energy for me. He demonstrated the positive and negative or shadow aspects for me. When caught up in the moment or experience I described earlier as essential, one can also lose sight of future possibilities.

My father died of suicide in August 1997. He was caught up in the moment of confusion and much despair. Without anyone else around, disconnected from others, alone in his house while his wife and two children were out shopping, he overdosed on medication meant to heal, not end his life.

I will always miss him. I miss him terribly, even as I write this.

Now, my partner Jose seems to manifest this lover's archetypal energy for me. Through both men, I have received the lessons of being connected, being present in the new experience, and allowing myself to feel my body and its senses.

Through this archetypal energy, I can better accept and connect with my sexuality and how it can enter the consulting room with my clients. Being aware and maintaining connections with others is important in the work.

I am thankful I had and still have, men who allowed this archetypal energy to flow through them and teach me. I'm also ever so thankful that I had an opportunity to put this book together and have you read its contents with the hope that my experience sounds familiar. May these words and pages offer you wisdom and hope on your journey. Being able to offer this to you is the greatest of blessings, truly.

Let's reflect:

What has moved you about this chapter on the lover archetype? What parts of your body did you feel the feelings you felt as you read this?

Who has been the lover archetype in your life? Maybe you have embodied this archetypal energy?

Any other thoughts, ideas, or emotions that came up as you read? What do they say to you?

Conclusion

Photo by Madeline Pere

In this book, I wanted to share how masculine archetypes have played out in my life through my relationships with my stepfather, uncle, father, and current partner. It has been an invaluable journey of self-discovery and individuation as I became aware of how these archetypal energies manifested through these men. This awareness has helped me confront painful memories and understand these men's roles in shaping my path in life.

Through a slow process of reflection, catharsis, and integration, I have grown stronger and more capable of embracing and embodying mature masculine archetypal energy. In my recent work, I've noticed that my practice has naturally focused on working with male clients, although I don't intentionally exclude women. It's just that currently, I mainly have male clients. These men often present a common theme—a longing for mature masculine energy, regardless of their sexual orientation. As I continue my work, I see more evidence of how crucial and urgent it is for men to reconnect with these essential energies for their personal growth and for the betterment of society.

By understanding and integrating mature masculine archetypal energies, I suggest we find balance and create a transcendent function that brings gay men closer to wholeness. The same applies to heterosexual men who may have rejected the masculine due to abusive or absent fathers, leaving them immature and dependent. This can be seen in their entitlement and lack of maturity. When heterosexual men reject mature masculine archetypal energy, they remain in the world of the mother and miss out on increased consciousness and growth. To progress into manhood, they need a father figure or someone to model mature masculine archetypal energy, which helps them establish and sustain a deeper connection with their inner masculine energy.

In this journey, embracing both the masculine and feminine aspects within ourselves is essential to finding balance and completeness. By integrating mature masculine energies, we can become more conscious, mature, and independent individuals, regardless of our sexual orientation. This process of inner transformation allows us to connect with our true selves, grow as individuals, and contribute positively to the world around us. Through this integration, we can achieve a higher state of wholeness and live more fulfilling lives.

I believe it is crucial for men, despite where they fall on the sexual orientation spectrum, to reconnect with mature masculine archetypal energies. This process is essential for men to find increased connection with their true selves, achieve integration, and attain a sense of wholeness.

It's the path I feel drawn to in my work, as I am called to serve all men, regardless of their sexual orientation. I see my role as walking alongside them on their journey of initiation and growth. By guiding them towards embracing the mature masculine within themselves, I aim to support their personal development and help them discover a deeper sense of purpose and fulfillment. This work holds immense value as it contributes to building stronger, more conscious, and empowered men who can positively impact their lives and the world around them.

In conclusion, I want to express my heartfelt gratitude to you, dear reader, for accompanying me on this journey as I explored the many milestones and landmarks of masculinity while attempting to impart some valuable lessons. Understanding our masculinity is a deeply personal and transformative process. I commend you for taking the time to delve into this subject with an open mind and a willing heart.

As you continue on your path, may you find the strength, wisdom, and compassion to embrace and define your masculinity on your terms. Wishing you the absolute best on this remarkable journey of self-discovery and growth. May you thrive, flourish, and become the best version of yourself.

Here's to a future filled with authenticity, self-awareness, and a profound understanding of what it truly means to be a man.

About The Author

Dr. R B Hernández-Cruz

DR. RB. HERNANDEZ INTEGRATES an extensive background in leadership transformation through the art and science of the spoken word and maintaining authentic charisma related to what Robert calls the *ego-Self Axis Leadership*.

Dr. RB Hernandez has been a licensed psychologist in private practice since 2005 and holds a Doctor of Psychology degree. He is licensed by the State of Florida Board of Psychologists.

He is a sought-after keynote speaker in Portuguese, Spanish, and English, where he keeps his passion for leadership development, training, and public education alive.

He considers himself a Galician-Cuban-American Soul carried within a farmer's heart, where he spends his days in the Ribeiro, along the Miño River in the land of his maternal heritage.

https://www.discoveringmyself.com